D1476894

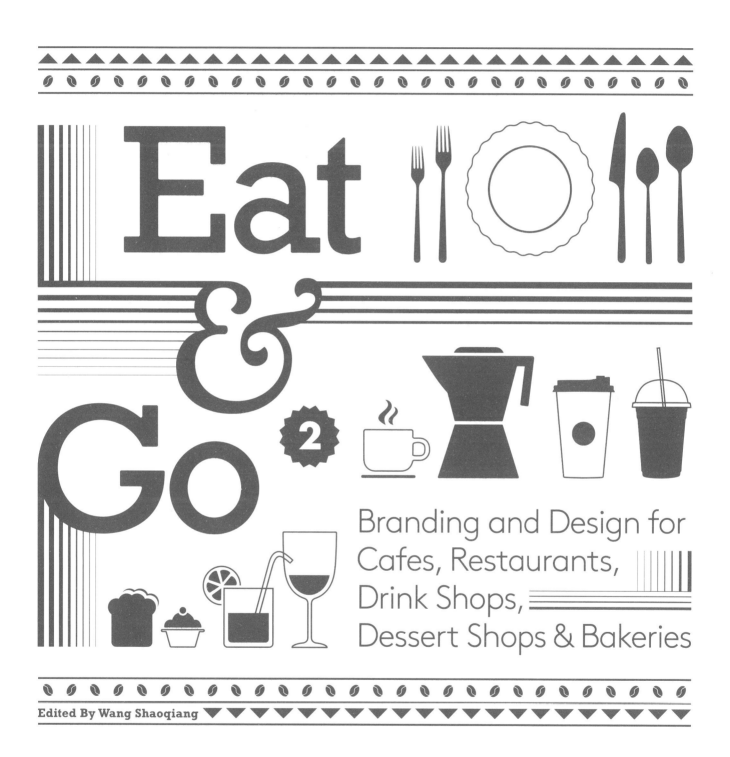

Eat & Go ②

Branding and Design for
Cafes, Restaurants,
Drink Shops,
Dessert Shops & Bakeries

Edited By Wang Shaoqiang

HOAKI

 HOAKI

Hoaki Books, S.L.
C/ Ausiàs March, 128
08013 Barcelona, Spain
T. 0034 935 952 283
F. 0034 932 654 883
info@hoaki.com
www.hoaki.com

hoaki_books

Eat & Go 2
Branding and Design for Cafes, Restaurants, Drink Shops, Dessert Shops
& Bakeries

ISBN: 978-84-17656-61-4

Copyright © 2022 by Sandu Publishing Co., Ltd.
Copyright © 2022 by Hoaki Books, S.L.
for sale in Europe and America

Sponsored by Design 360° — Concept & Design Magazine
Edited, produced, book design, concepts & art direction by
Sandu Publishing Co., Ltd.
info@sandupublishing.com
Chief Editor: Wang Shaoqiang
Executive Editor: Anton Tan
Copy Editor: Palmiche Press
Designer: Wu Yanting
Cover Design: Wu Yanting

D.L.: B 776-2022
Printed in China

Contents

Preface

....

The signature dishes, the perfect expresso blend, the award-winning latte art, the greenery venue interior, and the impeccable table service..., great food, delicious drinks, and service are an integral part of the eating and drinking experience. The hospitality branding and interior add an equally important ingredient to the mix. Good branding can provoke an emotional response, an ambience of inclusiveness, inflame delight, satisfaction, and even nostalgia.

There's an old saying, "if you cook good food, customers will come." However, good food is not enough. Customer perspectives and behaviour are changing. More is needed to attract them and to keep them coming back. Hospitality branding is like an entree—it's a visual taste of what to expect before they even savour what is served. Good brand design is essential for business. It attracts the patrons, gets them in the door, entices them, and keeps them wanting more. This overall experience is what keeps them coming back.

Design provokes an emotional response in us, whether it is a casual eatery, a traditional family-operated restaurant, a chic modern bakery, or a satisfying scene that we're in the know. Good branding gives that extra boost of confidence that helps to promote the business organically.

Of course, some local eating places that have never had good branding but still manages to serve customers for generations. Imagine, if they had good re-branding, they might attract more customers from far and wide. It can also create an efficient and satisfying working environment for staff.

The hospitality industry has rapidly changed how it operates in the advent of the COVID-19 epidemic. Many have adapted to this new normal, and their needs reflect this changing environment. As designers, we have to meet these new expectations. Menu design requirements are changing. Perhaps they need to be easy to clean, or a touch screen, an online ordering system, hands-free, or an overhead type of menu. Many restaurants and cafes are adding special takeaway menus to their regular offering. Some have specific packaging for takeaways.

....

It is important now more than ever to support your local business. There are plenty of ways to get behind your favourite food, beverage, and service business. Lockdown does not necessarily mean that you have more free time at home. For me, I have to juggle my work at home with my children. Buying takeaway from my favourite local restaurants does not just save my time, but I am supporting them as well. While you're there, perhaps leave your server a tip, even if it's just for a simple takeaway.

If you are too busy or just too lazy to shop for gifts during these pandemic times, then perhaps consider buying a gift voucher from your favourite hospitality business. Many businesses need cash to flow right now, so they can keep paying their bills and staff wages. Gift vouchers are a great way to help them. Even if they don't do gift vouchers, I think that it's worth asking them anyway. Who knows, it's likely that they've never considered that and may even make one.

Try to help them promote their business whenever you can post photos on your social media. A good branding helps to entice customers to snap a few photos to promote more of their brand. For the Instagram celebrities, influencers, or food bloggers, please don't ask for free meal in advertising returns. Only consider this if it's truly beneficial and fair to the business and not a self-serving measure for yourself. Please pay for the food and help promote them.

Since the pandemic, the hospitality industry has been changing. These are very challenging times. Despite many venues closing, competition is higher now more than ever, with many new venues popping up every day to take their places.

Good branding helps businesses to get noticed and will attract patrons.

Good branding is good for business.

Vian Risanto
Hue Studio

Cafes

Interview with **AguWu**

AguWu is a Polish graphic designer focusing on branding. She has been working in this field for around a decade and has developed her unique style based on minimal, geometric shapes and playful, yet elegant designs. Such an impactful style is versatile, so her clients span over multiple industries and she is able to accommodate diverse needs of their brands.

What do you think about the relationship between the cafe's brand design and its interior design?

AguWu: Everything should be connected. The printed materials, social media feeling, and interior design need to work together and be consistent. In PopUp Coffee Shop, you can see such a connection in every piece of branding. For example, the form of furniture refers to the shape of the logo. The branding pattern corresponds with the shape of the coffee mugs. The printed materials and colours are consistent with the whole interior. There is a strong relationship between the brand and the interior that should give you a specific feeling. That is why a cafe branding is a cooperation with the brand owner, interior designer, copywriter, web designer, etc. It is teamwork, and only good communication gives you a coherent, well-designed product.

In your opinion, what is a successful cafe brand design?

AguWu: A successful brand design is understandable. And it solves problems and challenges. It should be inviting and memorable, bringing the customer's attention and a promise that he/she can get something different from its competitor, something better. Branding should be functional and aesthetic. A customer wants to revisit a cafe, not only because of the coffee's taste but also the comfortable atmosphere inside. Then it is successful branding.

What is your working flow in brand design? How do you communicate with the client? How do you prepare for the preliminary work?

AguWu: If it is an individual client, a place with passion, family business, etc., but not a large company, I should meet in person. After accepting the terms of cooperation, I usually prepare a mood board with inspirations, sometimes preliminary sketches that I will show at the meeting. And we discuss what the client likes and dislikes. The client explains what feeling he/she wants to evoke with his brand, how customers should feel and how the brand should be perceived. A designer should direct the client in terms of design and technical possibilities. It is best if the client cooperates with the designer, then the brand is a joint project—it speaks to the client and is well designed by professional. Working with Bartosz on PopUp Coffee Shop branding was lots of fun to me. We became not only business partners for long but also good friends.

What are the difficulties in the cafe brand design? How did you solve them?

AguWu: At the first meeting, my client had a list of dreams he wanted to come true in his cafe. I knew from the beginning that the logo could become a neon sign, so I had it in my mind when I designed the outline PopUp Coffee Shop logotype. The cafe's external appearance was quite challenging. The place is so small that it had to pop. That is why I chose a non-standard

signboard shape, and we decided to paint the door bright yellow. But the most challenging turned out to be the COVID-19 epidemic right after the opening. The happy, comforting social media communication and bright brand colours were helpful. I designed stickers and labels for takeaway products to encourage people to come even if they cannot sit in the cafe and take a sip of coffee at home. It is always a good idea to design some additional elements of branding.

PopUp Coffee Shop, as your first designed cafe brand project, has received great attention. Could you share your design experience for this project?

AguWu: From the very beginning, I felt it would be a great project for me. After I read the short brief, I had my head full of ideas. Then I met my client, and an instant connection came out. Even if I didn't like some of his ideas, I tried to

be understanding and open to his vision. And it came out very nice in the end. So the most important thing is to work with the client on his vision and help him knit the pieces together. You also have to think about the cafe's customers and what feelings you want to evoke when they come in and contact the cafe brand.

Do you think that the demand for unique brand designs of cafes is increasing?

AguWu: I think that the demand for unique brand design is increasing in every industry. Everyone wants to stand out. I can see that my clients are bolder and want to have unique branding from head to toe. They are more aware that a logo is not enough. That applies even more to cafes. People want to experience special moments in a unique setting, especially in such a difficult time.

PopUp Coffee Shop

Cracow, Poland

Design **AguWu**

As a brand new coffee shop in Cracow, PopUp needs to have something different from other cafes at first glance, both in the business and visual identity. The colour of the whole brand is bright, candy, and sunny. The custom logo layout in the form of a pill on a yellow background is striking. The brand name presented in the form of a jug with a drop gives a signal that this is a cafe. The interior refers to branding—the rounded edges of the equipment and furniture, a pink coffee machine, and a large neon sign with the logo. People like PopUp. They like to be in such a cafe, talk to the passionate owner, and take a selfie with the neon sign. They are happy to take stickers and share photos on social media spreading the fame of PopUp among new customers. Appropriate design attracts young people, but it isn't childish, so that everyone will feel good there.

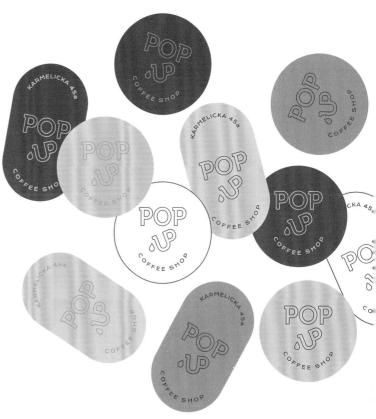

NO
SUGAR
NEEDED

@POPUP_COFFEESHOP

Mineral Cafe

Jakarta, Indonesia

Design Agency **Studio Woork** | Art Direction **Io Woo** | Design **Io Woo**
Architect **Studio Pppooolll (Kamil Muhammad)**

Inspired by nature, the designers designed the brand with an organic approach. The identity got inspired by the shape of mineral stone. The brand's personality maintains contrasts from shapes, typography, and colours that create a homey cafe. They also put thought into the logo identity to create a strong image and accentuate the brand while still giving a casual and welcoming look for the audience. All the collaterals and packaging for takeaway orders are also eco-friendly. They consist of paper bags, meal boxes, and plates. The materials used are kraft brown paper, recycled paper, clay, and cardboard with the cafe's identity.

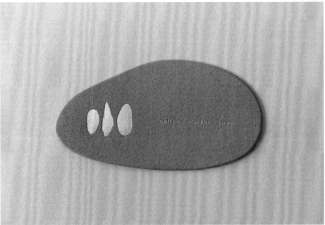

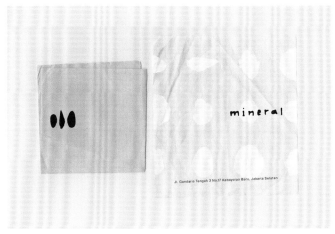

mineral

Jl. Gandaria Tengah 3 No.17 Kebayoran Baru, Jakarta Selatan

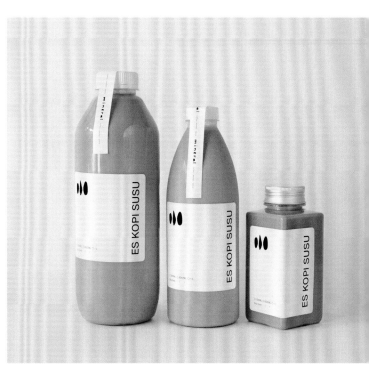

ES KOPI SUSU

ES KOPI SUSU

ES KOPI SUSU

Smoking Area

Prayer Room

Kitchen

Order Here

Private Room

Staff Only

Herbata i Kawa

Warsaw, Poland

Design **Aleksandra Lampart**
Collaboration **Walk with David**

Herbata i Kawa is a cafe, shop, and team room located in Warsaw. It is a friendly place with city energy, where people can not only do shopping, drink coffee, but also conduct workshops and training. The minimalist logo and branding are based on linear illustrations, displaying coffee and tea stories.

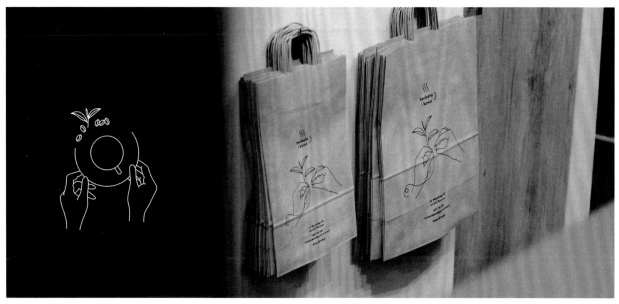

ACC

Seoul, South Korea

Design Agency **Studio IeM** | Design **Minseong Jeon**
Consultant **Seungyong Sun**

In the past, cafes in South Korea mostly focused on the quality of coffee than the atmosphere. However, they have gradually evolved as spaces where people can communicate, share ideas, and get inspired by each other. ACC (Archive Coffee Company) was created as a place where people build relationships. People began to build a relationship with other people in ACC, and at the same time, they were also building a relationship with the place itself. ACC's graphic motifs were found in the letters A and C. The designers observed the basic shape those letters have, and they created the visual identity through repetition and deformation of shapes. They have also created three different types of patterns using the basic shapes of letters in a simple and modern form. Meanwhile, they utilised those graphic elements in posters and other applications.

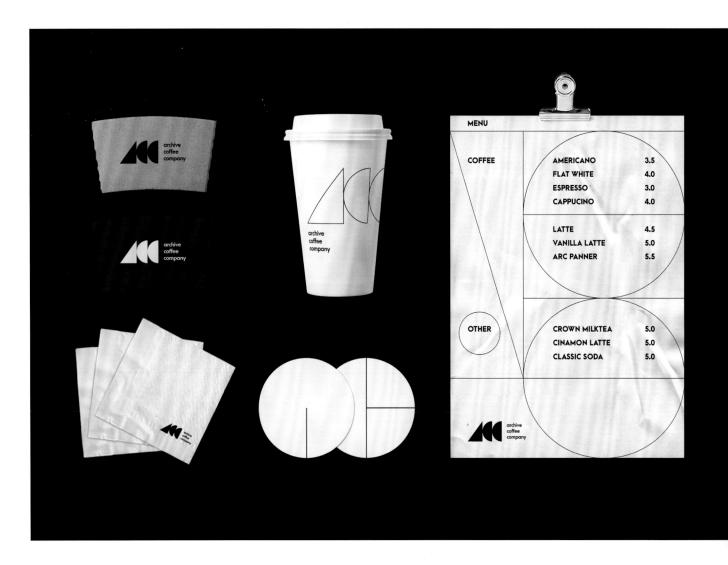

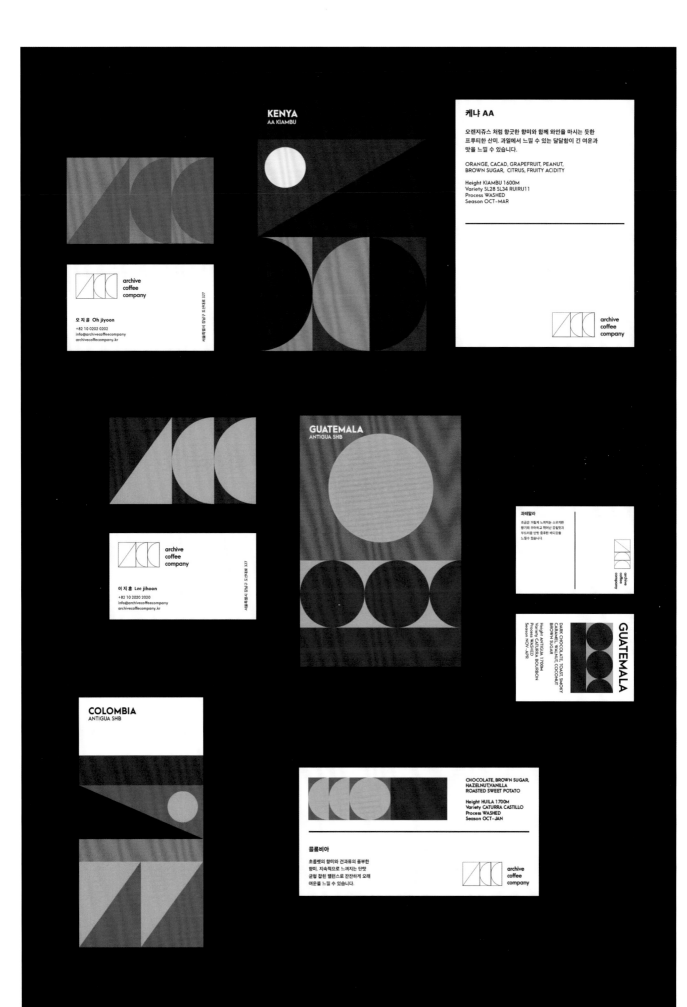

archive

coffee

archive coffee company

Archive Coffee Company is a special tea coffee roasting company.

Archive Coffee Company is a special tea coffee roasting company.

company

archive
coffee
company

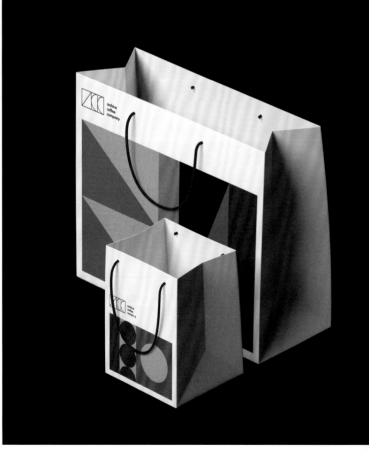

TU7UHARI

Jakarta, Indonesia

Design Agency \\' Brand Agency | Design Michael Kristiantowi, Sisiana Pradita, Wildan Ilham
Photography Bernico Christianto, Genny Furqiza, Stephanus Mering

TU7UHARI approached the design team for optimising their branding, concept, visual identity system, and development. They focused on the TU7UHARI's founders' idealism that work-life balance is, indeed, not for everyone. It becomes a perfect match for a segment they termed as "highly productive millennials," the go-getters for goals and dreams who are unbound by the nine-to-five rule. They, therefore, decided to use this idea as their stepping stone. Mentioned by *Manual Jakarta*, TU7UHARI became one of the new favourite coffee places in Jakarta. Such a newcomer created a disruptive distinctiveness in a quite saturated market and even more.

PROJECT Sangrai 1.0

Jakarta, Indonesia

Design Agency **Studio Woork** | Design **Io Woo, Danang Abiyoso**
Client **Kopikalyan**

PROJECT Sangrai is a project initiated by Kopikalyan where people, especially coffee enthusiasts, can collaborate and inspire each other whilst promoting coffees in Indonesia to a bigger market in their way. The logo identity design for PROJECT Sangrai 1.0 was inspired by the rotating movement of a coffee roasting machine. The packaging for PROJECT Sangrai 1.0 comes in the shape of a box with easy pulling access that holds two bags of Kopikalyan high-quality ground coffee beans. The designers used a pop of blue colour for the branding concept of PROJECT Sangrai 1.0 to respond to the muted earth tones of Kopikalyan's cafe environment, creating a fresh look that seeks attention at the same time.

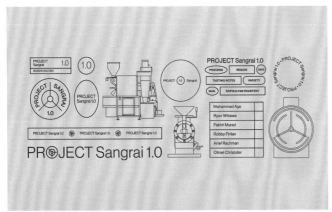

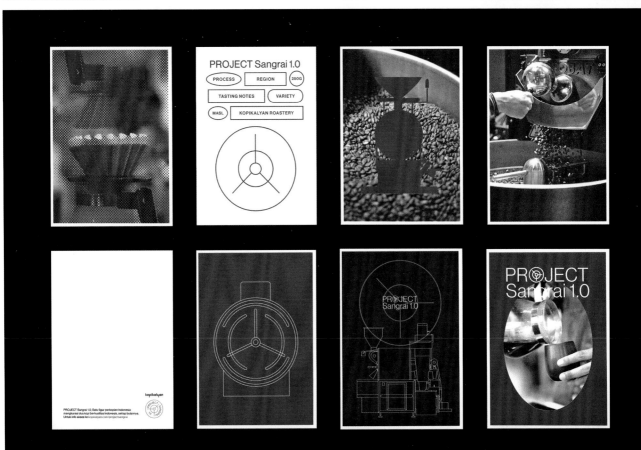

Prospect Coffee Roasters

Ventura, USA

Design Agency **Alter** | Design Direction **Jonathan Wallace**
Design **Symon McVilly, Jonathan Wallace, Shaun Manyweathers, Sam Phillips**
Illustration **Symon McVilly**

Prospect is a tribute to a unique American swathe of typographic brands that rapidly evolved and were codified throughout the 20th century. It is a mix of bold typographies and relaxing illustrations that combine for a strong but unpretentious characteristic that is beautifully suited to its laid-back home in Ventura, California. This brand has been chosen and promoted across various international channels, which began as packaging and expanded into a new identity which streamlined various aspects of communication. The creation of laid-back and friendly culture is the key to the success of this project.

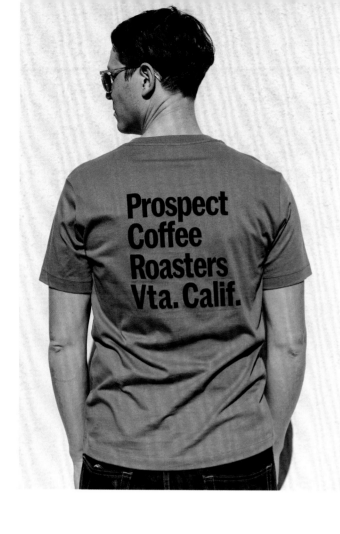

Lights in the Attic

Melbourne, Australia

Design Agency **Hue Studio** | Creative Direction **Vian Risanto**
Design **Vian Risanto, Adela Saputra**

This cafe branding was inspired by the name "Lights in the Attic." The whole nuance of the branding resembles lights that fall on wall surfaces. With custom lettering, Hue Studio created a logotype that is clean and simple yet unique. Lights in the Attic celebrates materiality in a raw and finished form. From the raw steel bleeds to a mirror polish, a sandblasted wall is draped with denim, and a polished ceiling draws the eye from an exposed concrete slab. They translated that philosophy to the stamping coffee cups and raw boxboard material that were used for menu and loyalty cards.

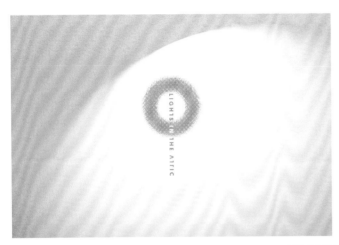

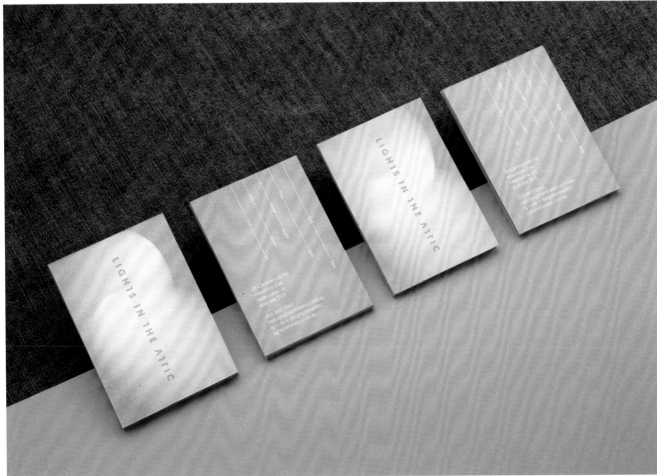

Story Espresso

Sydney, Australia

Design Agency **For The People** | Creative Direction **Jason Little**
Design Direction **Olivia King, Kinal Ladha** | Design **Pete Conforto, Chris Van Niekerk**
Copywriting **Mat Groom, Daniel St. Vincent** | Illustration **Ilana Bodenstein**

Story Espresso celebrates coffee's foundational role in life's stories, by using every point of interaction as a jumping-off point into a new type of story. A conversation over the flat white might become a love affair, for example, or a croissant might become the treasured prize to fight over. And as each new story enfolds, the designers show their respect to the legacy of storytelling, by exploring various forms (like *haikus*, screenplays, and branching narratives) or library-esque loyalty cards.

The enigmatic monster character watches over the proceedings, representing the great unknown of stories yet to be told, and illustration collaborations allow the brand to explore non-verbal storytelling from non-traditional perspectives on limited-edition packaging and merchandise.

Clearly
this was
a sign.

Story
4 Gamma Rd
Lane Cove, NSW 2066
ABN 84 638 877 048
PURCHASE

13 Dec 2020
10:48 am

Authorisation 389399
Receipt ZlyU

Visa DEBIT
AID A0 00 00 00 03 10 10
Verified by Device

$14.00

250g Bean *
story house blend

$14.00
$14.00

Total
Visa 9329 (Contactless)

You stash the receipt into your wallet. You
tell yourself you'll use it for your tax return.
Obviously you won't. You will, however, in
three months time, long after the ink has
faded, use it to jot down a stranger's phone
number. And then, you'll call it. And meet
again with them. And fall for them. And leave
the country for them. And fight with them,
late one night, with tears in your eyes,
And, late one night, with tears in your eyes,
leave them. But, you'll continue to think of
them. And each time, every single time, you'll
smile – and hope, wherever they are, they're
happy.

NON-TAXABLE ITEM *

TAX INVOICE

Later today, you'll be lying in the middle of a dusty, deserted street – paying the price
for being the *second-fastest six-shooter in Lane Cove*. In your final moments, Ringo will
ask you if it was all worth it. Risking your life, for a croissant. And with your final words,
you'll whisper: *"Yes. Because it wasn't any croissant. It was a Penny Fours croissant."*

STORY & Penny Fours

The ship's computer lurches you out of a cold, dreamless hypersleep. You stumble out
of the cryogenic bath, a rug draped around you by one of the company's medidroids.
Your vitals are checked. Other members of the crew begin to wake. You sit down in the
mess, to your first meal in 35,424 days: lab prepared nutrient sludge. You lower your
spoon and think back to your days on Earth, knowing you'll never have an Iggy's
sourdough loaf again.

STORY & Iggy's

You only have a few seconds. You run your fingers across the painting's frame, finding
the lever. The safe clunks open. A dossier, a pearl necklace... and a *fake*. Ms. Stevens
returns from the bathroom, having slipped into "something a little more comfortable".
In her porcelain hands, a svelte handgun, in the other... *the prize*. "Darling. You didn't
think I'd stupid enough to leave the real Shortstop vanilla bean donut just lying
about the place, did you?"

STORY & Shortstop

LANE COVE   SYDNEY

We OPEN on a
simple sandwich board.
It sweats under its hinges,
as it desperately spruiks
the specials of the day.

As the street lamps light,
it folds up, and heads
inside for another night
alone in the broom closet.

STORY

VOLUME 01 / EDITION 05

A Stranger Comes to Town
– *Single Origin [Filter]*

You were seated a couple of rows in front of me.
I didn't see you at first, didn't think to look — after all,
it was the same old Sunday crowd... except for you.
Sitting alone. Bathed in screen light. When you laughed,
I couldn't help but smile. When you curled up into
your seat, I would scan the screen intently, hoping to
understand what struck a chord within you. And when
you stood up to leave, every part of me wanted to call
out, to ask you to share a coffee with me, to share a book,
to share a trip to Barcelona, or Vis — where, like in the
movies, we'd realise our home had been there, all along,
waiting for us...! Instead... I remained frozen. And you
walked into the night. I returned the next week, and
the week after that — but I never saw you again. I'll be
there every Sunday, though. I promise. And if you ever
do return... I hope, this time, I won't freeze.

ORIGIN: *Ethiopia*

Sister Cafe

Brisbane, Australia

Design Agency **Autumn Studio**

Autumn Studio designed the brand and illustrations for Sister, a cafe based in Hawthorne, Brisbane, serving speciality coffee and food. The identity features fun, quirky illustrations that are cafe-themed. They consist of familiar objects with an interesting twist to inspire and delight. The owner of Sister relied on Autumn Studio to consistently create a strong brand identity. And the result is surprising and beyond expectation with both branding concepts and how Autumn Studio brought the brand to life.

NMA CAFE

Taiwan, China

Design **Lung-Hao Chiang** | Copywriting **Lung-Hao Chiang**

The designer considered that coffee shops on the market generally use all white or all black and metallic colours as the main colour, which lacks a sense of relaxation and humour. Therefore, he chose a refreshing and bright colour scheme for NMA CAFE to create a clean and thorough brand personality. In terms of the visual strategy, the designer hopes to give NMA CAFE a symbol suitable for various extended applications and strong memory points. At the same time, the designer intends to keep innocent playfulness in the brand image, so he uses illustrations to interpret a coffee imaginary space. And each coffee flavour has its own characteristic, allowing customers to enjoy it.

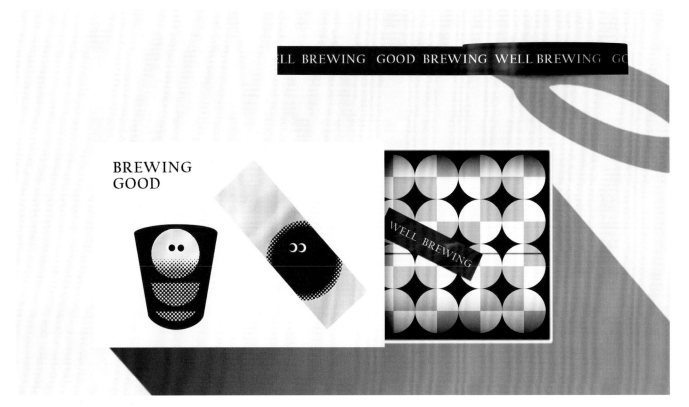

The Lab Coffee & Co.

Wuxi, China

Design Agency **HDU23 Lab** | Art Direction **Wu Siguang**
Design **Wu Siguang, Wong Ka-Ho**

The Lab Coffee & Co. is a boutique cafe focusing on coffee taste test and experience. To put the experience of coffee itself first, the designers weakened the brand logo and name. Instead, they designed the graphics serving the coffee brewing method, taste, and smell perception as a visual recognition system for the cafe.

The composition of this set of graphics is based on black and white language, echoing the experimental themes of fusion and exclusion and conveying the characteristics of coffee and coffee beans to the audience in multiple dimensions through the association of vision, taste, and smell.

GRAPHICS OF COFFEE TYPES:

ESPRESSO

AMERICANO

LATTE

FLAT WHITE

CAPPUCCINO

MOCHA

COLD BREW

GRAPHICS OF COFFEE BEAN FLAVORS:

FLOWERS

FRUITS

BAKING

HERBACEOUS

ALCOHOL

CHOCOLATE

SPICE

NUTS

SUGAR

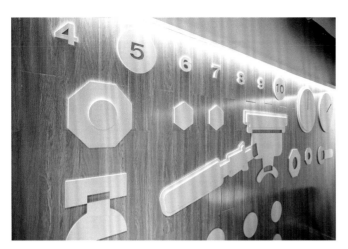

ORDER & CASHIER

THE COFFEE LAB

Granger

Melbourne, Australia

Design Agency **Both** | Design **Sigiriya Brown, Dan Smith**
Interior Design **Kate Lee** | Photography **Shelley Horan** | Client **Nick Gardiner**

Named for Grange Road on which the restaurant sits, Both was tasked with creating an approachable identity for Granger with enduring relaxed elegance. Both worked closely with interior designer Kate Lee throughout the project to develop a visual identity that would become a part of the fabric of the space. To ensure that the identity is harmonious with the materials and colours used in the interior scheme, Both chose a palette of cream and warm white, punctuated with the signature green used in the fit-out. Both also utilised understated finishes, such as white foiling, to echo the confident restraint of the space.

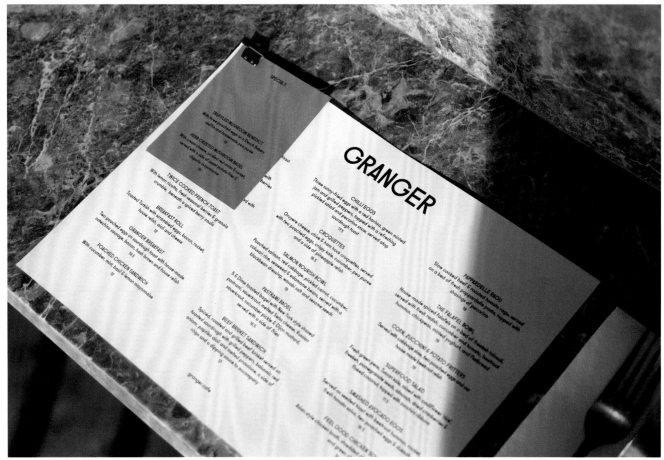

Retrograde Coffee

Nashville, USA

Design **Perky Bros** | Photography **Nicola Harger, Brett Warren**

MW Real Estate Group decided to build up a coffee shop as an office environment. Retrograde is a cosy "coffee stop" nestled into Nashville's east side that's dedicated to providing the neighbourhood with a welcoming spot to slow down and press pause for a moment on the daily path.

Taking cues from the name, the visual identity gets inspired by the cosmic phenomenon of retrograde motion, especially the moment when the Mercury appears to hover and begin to move backwards. The reverse italic logotype features three custom sputnik-like "R"s with geometric counters referencing the Mercury, Earth, and Sun. The brand symbol pulls them together in a simple interstellar monogram. And the calm colour palette is complemented with a touch of bright gold fit for a NASA satellite.

CAFE 3/92

Mexico City, Mexico

Art Direction, Design & Illustration **Karla Heredia**
Photography **Felipe Hedding**

CAFE 3/92 is a cafe located in Mexico City with an outgoing and fun personality. The key visual is a sluggard fox who enjoys drinking a lot of coffee and wanders everywhere. The designer aimed to use and reproduce the identity in multiple applications, giving strength to the key visual and liven up the environment.

COFFEEMARSH

Fuzhou, China

Design Agency **Temperature up up up**
Design **Liang Jia**

Initially, the owner struggled with which brand name is better—COFFEEMARSH or MARSHCOFFEE. It is a pleasure to display those two names together, just like the presentation of an inverted sentence. The design team chose to use the swap symbol (∏), which is used to exchange the positions of adjacent words in Chinese grammar proofreading. Meanwhile, that symbol also means depth and infinite extension.

ORANGE COFFEE

Düsseldorf, Germany

Design Agency & Art Direction **Design Studio B.O.B.** | Interior Design **Bianca Timmermann**
Photography **Pia Korani (Food), Marc Oortman (Interior)**

The name ORANGE in this coffee place refers not only to the coffee's colour when being held against the light but also to an Australian town famous for coffee. Therefore, the coordinates of that town are one of the main elements of the branding. The key element is the illustration of a coffee plant which was inspired by the old biological graphics showing the different growth phases and anatomy of a plant. A variety of brand elements and logos allow a flexible use for different applications. The design team successfully created a mix between the modern and the traditional and created a 360° experience for the young and the old.

Daechung Park

Seoul, South Korea

Design Agency **studio fnt**
Art Direction **Jaemin Lee**
Graphic Design **Jaemin Lee, Hyunsun You**
Space Design **FHHH Friends**
Furniture Design **studio COM**
Print **Corners**

This is a brand identity and graphic design work for Daechung Park, a cafe in Seoul. The word in their name "Daechung" means "half-heartedness" in Korean. After investigating further on the word "Daechung," the designers learned that in the old days of Asia, tigers used to be called "Daechung." It is a homonym made up of Chinese characters, meaning "Big Bug (Dae Chung)." The designer decided to use this concept to reveal an image of a tiger metaphorically in the overall design and story behind the cafe's identity.

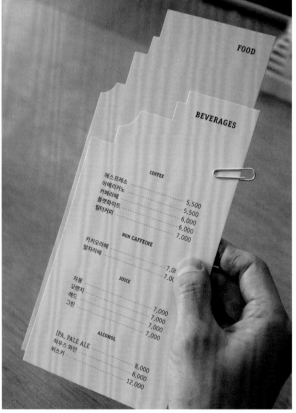

Moka Clube

Curitiba, Brazil

Design Agency **Pedro, Pastel & Besouro** | Creative Direction **Eduardo Rosa, Gustavo Caboco**
Design **Dora Suh, Felipe Lui, Fernanda Corrêa, Lucia Angélica, Rafael Ancara**

The coffee brand Moka Clube asked the design team to create a new visual identity. They extracted and mixed the elements of the Brazilian urban and countryside. They captured the rural essence of the farms and sheds where the coffee is processed. The illustrative icons allude to those elements presented in the country lifestyle, creating an illustration pack that expresses the true art of coffee making. Meanwhile, the modern font exclusively for Moka Clube contrasts organicity and geometry and displays elements used in the coffee industry branding at the beginning of the 20th century.

Low Grass

Athens, Greece

Design Agency **Luminous Design**

In the motherland of coffee, Ethiopia, drinking coffee is a ritual. During the ritual the coffee is prepared traditionally, roasted in a pan over a charcoal grill, while the surrounding is filled with sparse grass for people to sit on it. That's how the designers came up with the name and visual identity for Low Grass. The colour palette that rules the brand's visual identity accomplishes an unique story, whereas reflecting the energy and optimism emerging from a single cup of coffee. That calls for an customer to seek the adventure out of everyday life and love all things special.

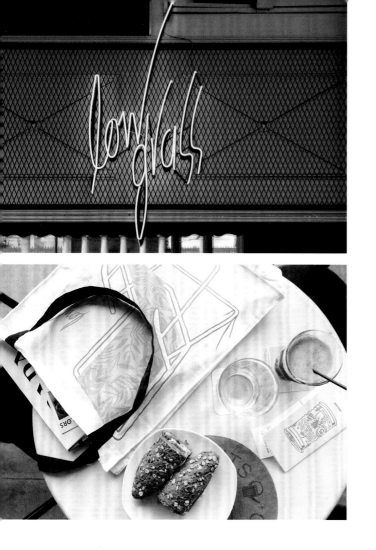

CAFE by MIMINKO

Seoul, South Korea

Design Agency **Tangible Design** | Creative Direction **Yoonseuk (Allen) Shim**
Design **Seohee Min**

The pet products brand MIMINKO newly launched a pet cafe. Tangible took charge of developing a new brand identity for it. The task was to create a comfortable space optimised for pets that use environment-friendly materials for the pets. The calligraphy, hand-drawing, and natural colour were used to express a harmonious atmosphere where pets can freely roam. The colours of the parent brand MIMINKO were used to establish consistency and uniformity of the brand.

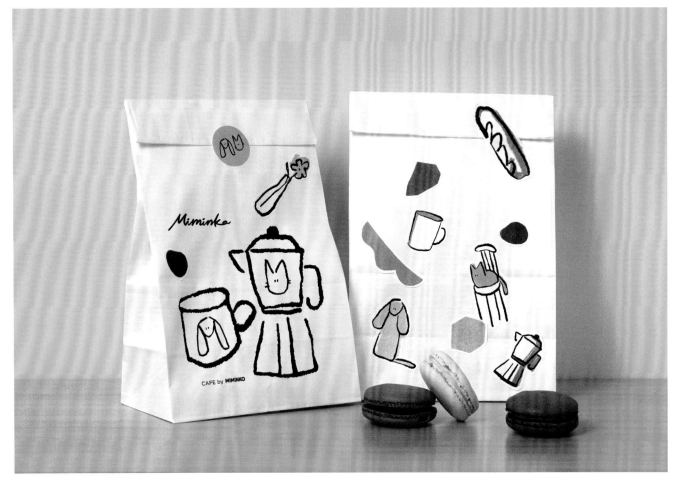

Ganso Cafe

Cancún, Mexico

Design **Karla Hernández (Charlötte)**
Client **Sofia Gutiérrez, COCAY**

Ganso Cafe is a cafeteria that offers a cool space for all ages—an ideal place to visit at any time of the day for those who like good coffee. Inspired by a tropical environment and a nearby playground, the designer sought a cheerful, childlike, and subtly elegant style.

Restaurants

Interview with **Human**

Human is an independent design firm founded by Alejandro Flores in 2016. This strategic design studio has skills and experience to bring focus and clarity to each brand identity.

Mexican catering industry is relatively developed. What kind of restaurant brand design do you think can play a role in attracting customers and enhancing competitiveness?

Alejandro Flores: Mexican catering industry is well-developed. We have several top-notch restaurants and bars in the 50 Best List and one of the best chefs in the world—Enrique Olvera. Overall, that is an exciting growing competitive scene. I believe the key to success in this growing market is to have a very well-crafted differentiation applied to food concept, branding, and interior design.

Human has participated in the brand design of many restaurants. What do you think is your biggest advantage?

Alejandro Flores: We have now more than 38 restaurants under our belt. We have come a long way. We believe very firmly in creating eye-catching concepts that tell a story. And we work side by side with architects and interior designers to create a thoroughly well-crafted design approach that covers the entire restaurant experience, from their first point of contact to the final bite.

How do you communicate with your clients? How to make them agree with your design?

Alejandro Flores: First of all, we have to know the clients very well—their goals and ambitions, what they have in mind, and overall, what their vision is. It is crucial to have constant communication with the clients to deliver what they expect.

Following getting to know the clients, every design approach has to be very well-built. The design has to be an equilibrium of how it works and how it looks. So if we have a very well-structured design with a solid strategy behind it, it will help the client see a good direction we are going in.

A menu is an important introduction to a restaurant, and it is also a tiny part of the brand design. It involves layout, typography, and other design elements. Could you share the experience of menu design, taking the Olenna project as an example?

Alejandro Flores: The entire branding experience must be unique; the concept must be present in the whole restaurant experience. For Olenna, we created a menu based on the ancient Roman Twelve Tables to continue with the Mediterranean storytelling. These menus were tailor-made for the restaurant, so they are instantly recognisable, give a higher-end feeling that any other restaurant can't provide. Therefore, it's about being memorable.

How do you think the restaurant brand design is coordinated with the spatial design to enhance the customer experience?

Alejandro Flores: It has to be a must. We have to remember that branding is the entire brand value. McDonald's would not be McDonald's without its interior design, as well as other famous brands.

The brand vision has to be complete and extensive. We must create spaces that communicate the uniqueness of the restaurant. We also have to keep the power of the digital world in mind. Many restaurants become viral by the photos that are taken of the place and uploaded to social media. So we must create unique spots recognisable that work as a part of the brand assets.

In the background of the COVID-19 epidemic, the food delivery industry is booming. What new challenges bring to the restaurant brand design?

Alejandro Flores: The biggest challenge is to transform the restaurant's offline experience into an on-the-go experience. Many of our clients are migrating to satisfy the demand of their customers but from their home. Even though the restaurant is coming back to normal, we have still reduced capacity in most restaurants, so to survive, we have to look for other ways of offering, such as apps. Meanwhile, we are aware of the challenge—it comes from ordering to you at home, but overall it does not matter if you eat at the restaurant or eat at home. The experience must be very similar.

Olenna

Mexico City, Mexico

Design Agency **Human** | Interior Design **Niz+Chauvet**
Photography **C129 Studio**

For the Olenna identity, Human took inspiration found in the three crops of Mediterranean agriculture—wheat, vine and olive, which give the three products of traditional food in that area—bread, wine and olive oil, also known as the Mediterranean Triad. The isotype created a simple yet strong link with the robust Mediterranean cuisine. In terms of the colour palette, they got inspired by a harmonious blend with blue and brown in Mediterranean culture. The logotype, constructed from a serif typeface, was specially conceived to look like types found in antique marble chisel engraving found in the area.

Overall, they created a relaxing atmosphere, full of plants and warm colours that stand out throughout the place and among the main points of interest. Olenna can captivate customers in all the senses with its comfort, beautiful terrace, and impeccable food created by the renowned chef Maycoll Calderón.

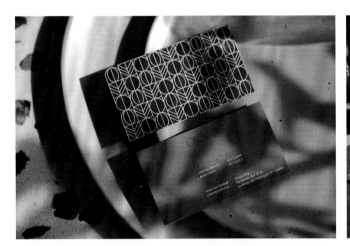

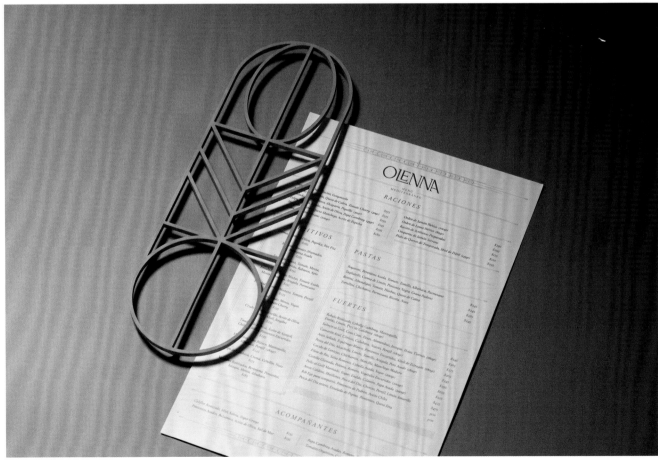

Pipiris Fries

Mexico City, Mexico

Design Agency **Manifiesto Mx**
Photography **Manifiesto Mx**

Pipiris Fries is a dark kitchen in Mexico City, one of the few places where people can get loaded fries. The founders wanted a brand that can capture the eccentric essence of their products that add a special touch to the fries, which makes anyone drool just by reading the menu. The identity helped Pipiris Fries instantly connect with their customers on a deeper level. The logo and mascot stuck in the customers' minds, creating a love mark that they want to keep close to them. It translates into better sales and a higher buyback rate.

casa müi

Mexico City, Mexico

Design Agency **VVORKROOM**
Strategy **Checo Gutiérrez, Juanjo Saldívar**
Photography **Common Matter, Rodrigo Chapa**

"Casa" means house in Spanish, and "Müi" means heart in Otomi (an indigenous language of the central region of Mexico). With the name, the designers wanted to refer to the fact that the kitchen in Mexico is the centre of everything. The graphic identity was inspired by the Otomi art and their colorful embroideries of organic figures. The designers worked on the three pillars that are the basis of all events: "the house" that represents the restaurant, "the heart" that represents the chef, and "the root" that represents the city where the pop-up will take place.

RESTAURANTE CASA
CHEF PAÍS O CIUDAD
EN CIUDAD

casa müi

OSSO CASA
RENZO GARIBALDI PERÚ
EN CIUDAD DE MÉXICO

casa müi

MANHATTA

New York, USA

Design Agency **Mucca** | Creative Direction **Matteo Bologna**
Design Direction **Andrea Brown** | Design **María Silva Mora**

MANHATTA is located high above the city on the 60th floor with some of the best views of New York City. Mucca created a brand strategy and design system aligned with the sophistication of the interior design and the quality of food, but still accessible, containing elements of wit, curiosity, and playfulness.

MANHATTA's approachable brand personality opens up the audience pool to not only the wealthy financial crowd of the area, but also to any types of local visitors or tourists that is in the mood for a fun and casual time.

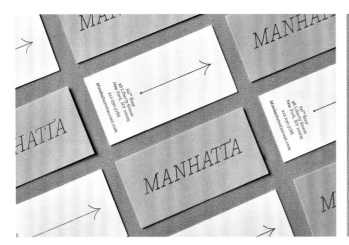
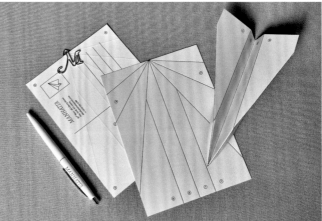

Old Friend

Adelaide, Australia

Design & Illustration **The Colour Club** | Photography **Josh Geelen**

Old Friend is a casual bar and eatery. True to its name, it's the perfect place to meet for any occasion, coffee, lunch, or cocktails. From the outset, the design team wanted the brand to feel equally familiar and comforting, like a secret handshake with one's best friend. A cheeky brand mark, nostalgic colour palette, and speckled patterns sit playfully across print collateral, held together with a structured type-set. Meanwhile, they created a set of nonsensical handshakes that grace the walls in the large open dining area. The restaurant became instantly popular amongst locals and developed a mass following in a short time.

SIGNATURE

- OLD FRIEND: genever, beer
  syrup, lemon juice, egg white,
  dash bitter creole pinpall

- PARESI: lagavulin giuliano,
  syrup, orange zest, bitter,
  chocolate, angostura

- THE TRAVELLER: white rum, dark
  rum, passion fruit, syrup, basil,
  lime, orange, angostura, soda

- HONEY I'M HOME: honey, dark
  rum / bourbon, lime, st germain

- VAN GOGH: hendricks, st
  germain, noilly prat white
  vermouth, sage bitter

- EL DIABLO: dark rum agrostion
  with cinnamon and habanero
  chilli, lime juice, sage

COCKTAILS MENU — ALL $18

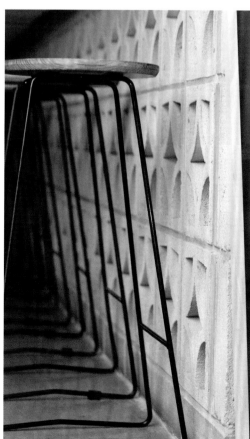

Don Tuch

Mexico City, Mexico

Design Agency **Human** | Photography **C129 Studio**

The gastronomic tradition from Yucatán, is taken towards an eclectic concept combining authentic flavours memorably and uniquely. Don Tuch is a tribute to Yucatán cuisine in a playful and relaxed approach. For the brand's identity, Human wanted to create contrast between vintage and nostalgia playfully. They used a serif typeface and a vibrant colour palette to convey balance. They also created a character named Don Tuch to echo the whole brand. The reproduction of the branding assets is very important, so they created different sets of stickers and stamps. The result is a unique and friendly approach that welcomes every member of the family to enjoy this delicious food in a more relaxing ambience.

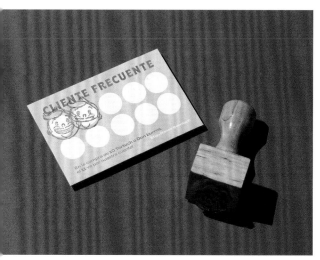

Subito

Madrid, Spain

Design Agency **Atipo**®

Subito promoters wanted to transmit the authentic Italian flavours, share a quality product, and change the concept of fast food equal to low-quality food. The challenge for the designers was to move away from the supposed artisan references to create a strong and distinctive concept that does not betray the commitment to a product with a long tradition and high quality. Subito means "immediately" in Italian. It is an energetic and vibrant name with a young audience in mind, a reflection of Italian nature, and a direct reference to the spirit of a business based on agile and street-side consumption. The designers created an imagotype that arises from the fusion of the synthesised image of two pizza slices and the fast-forward button icon.

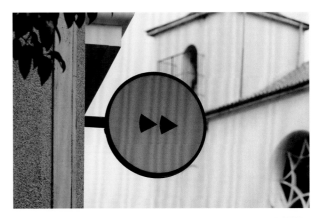

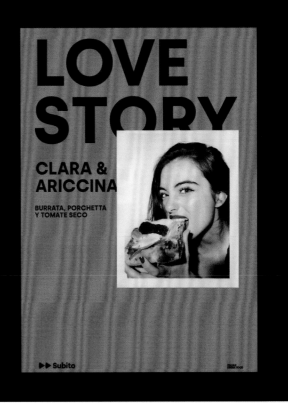

Counterpart

Los Angeles, USA

Design Agency **Asís** | Creative Direction **Raphael Farsat (Truffl)**
Art Direction & Design **Francisco Andriani, Clara Fernández (Asís)** | Client **Truffl**

Counterpart is a Los Angeles all-day brunch and coffee shop in Echo Park, serving delicious plant-based comfort food. Sitting on the corner of Echo Park Ave. and Delta St., Counterpart is where the corner deli meets the trendy modern cafe.

Counterpart's brand identity blends Eastside LA urban coolness with an organic, homey neighbourhood cafe feel. Asís used a simple black-and-white colour palette and minimalistic layouts to counterbalance the colorful, vibrant restaurant space and menu items. They designed a custom pattern inspired by the unique tiles in the restaurant, and hand-drawn illustrations using a human, natural, and imperfect style meant to align with the brand's neighbourhood atmosphere and the organic, natural ingredients used on the menu.

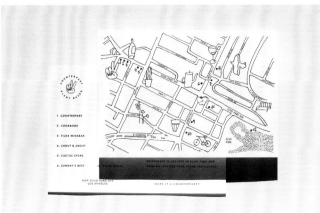

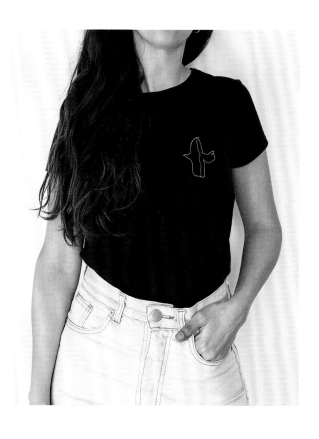

Chilaritos

Mexico City, Mexico

Design Agency **Manifiesto Mx**

Chilaritos is a restaurant in Mexico City, specialising in a typical Mexican meal chilaquiles, a popular cuisine elaborated with fried corn tortilla pieces and accompanied by spicy sauce and cheese. For the visual identity, the designers took inspiration from Mesoamerican elements and Mexican pop culture to reinterpret them with a contemporary touch and thus generate their own language within the brand development that feels fun and casual.

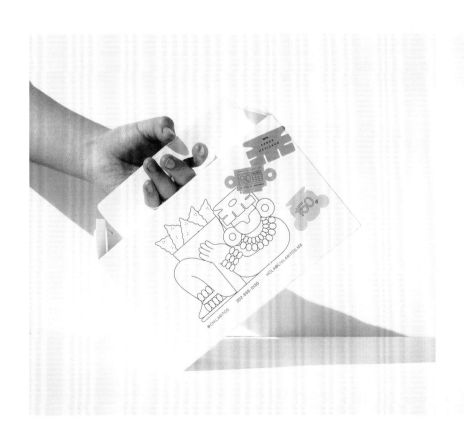

Fugu Fish Bar

Melbourne, Australia

Design Agency **Hue Studio** | Creative Direction **Vian Risanto** | Design **Vian Risanto, Vina Nurina**

Fugu Fish Bar is a new take on the Australian classic—fish and chips. The designers came up with the name *fugu* (pufferfish in Japanese), a delicacy in Japan. The designers wanted to create a different take on the common fish and chops branding. The weird and wonderful shapes of *fugu* are where the designers drew the graphic inspiration from. With the Riso printing technique, they created this edgy, fun, and colourful branding.

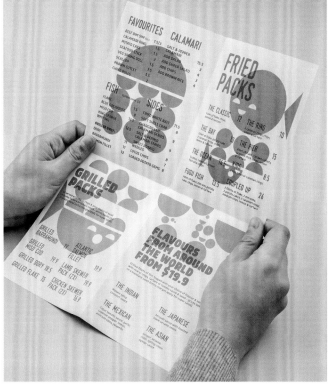

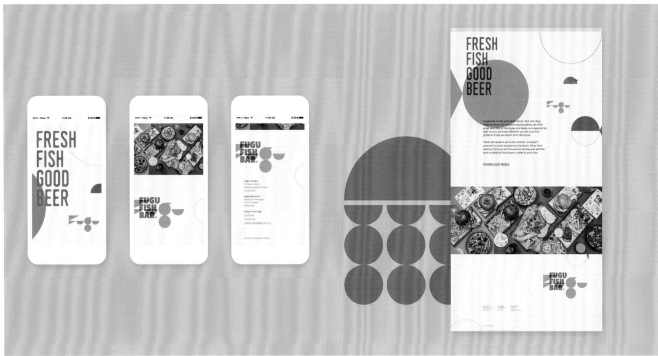

The Front Room

Jakarta, Indonesia

Design Agency **Thinking Room** | Creative Direction **Eric Widjaja** | Art Direction **Ritter Willy Putra**
Design **Clifford Caleb Dione** | Photography **Vony Wong**

The Front Room is a dining establishment inspired by the idea of utmost hospitality, similar to having guests over with a host passionate and attentive about the food, beverage, and ambience. A host needs to ensure guests with goodwill to have the most pleasant experience in his home is common. And the practice of serving flavour of favour was to be translated extensively through identity, packaging, and environmental design. With the concept refining the centuries-old tradition of hospitality, the designers adapted the story of Baucis and Philemon, who had disguised-gods Zeus and Hermes as guests in their humble home, providing them with courteous hospitality. The pitcher and goose in favour of their story became elements incorporated into an invitingly-amiable approach for the identity development, added with an arch representing a home—a charming symbol of shelter and safety.

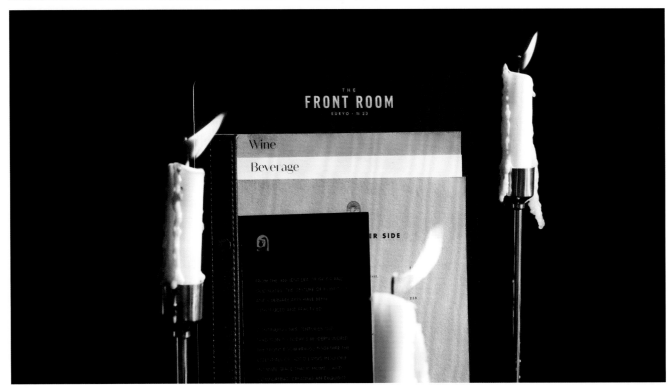

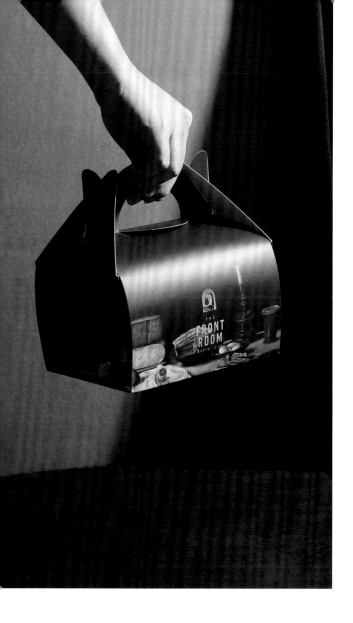

PÁULINE

Brooklyn, USA

Design **Louis Ngo**

The logo of PÁULINE was custom-drawn, according to the luxurious serif typeface. The letter U in PÁULINE was inspired by Poseidon's trident, meaning the variety and freshness of seafood from the deep sea. The array strokes in each character of PÁULINE are simulated as undulating waves and create rhythm in the logo. The dark green represents elegance, coolness, and mystery.

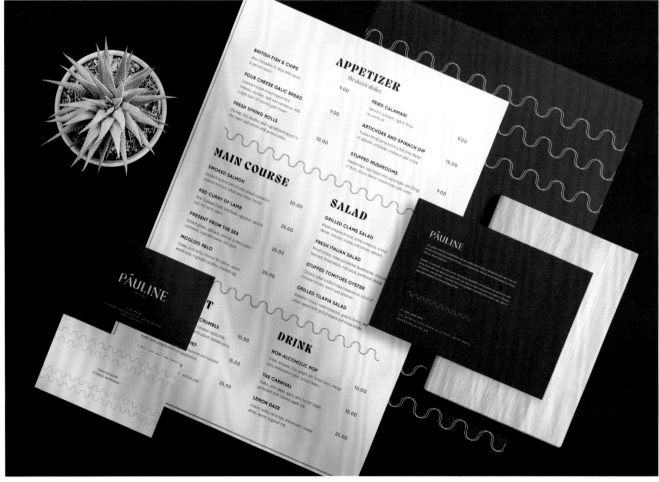

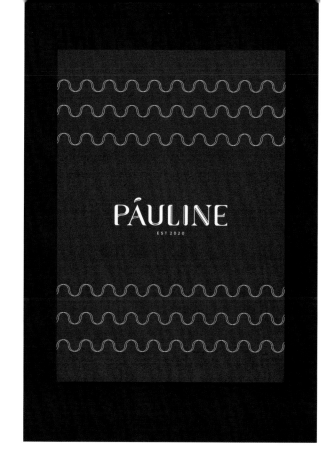

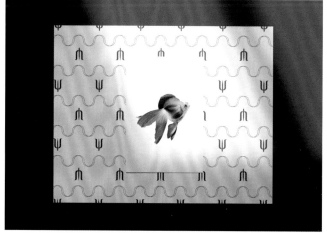

Bellavia Rebranding

Dubai, UAE

Design **Giovanni Borde** | Copywriting **Gavin Stradi**

Bellavia is a traditional Italian family-owned restaurant and bakery originally from Sicily and Napoli. Backed up by its family recipes and traditional Italian cuisine, the brand delivers on its promise of a very authentic experience without being cliche. Giovanni Borde used many Italian elements in the Bellavia rebranding, such as the architectures, street signages, and the tone of voice to show the nostalgic and authentic Italian lifestyle.

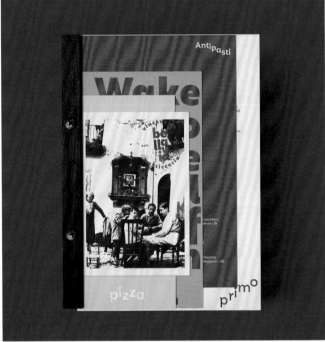

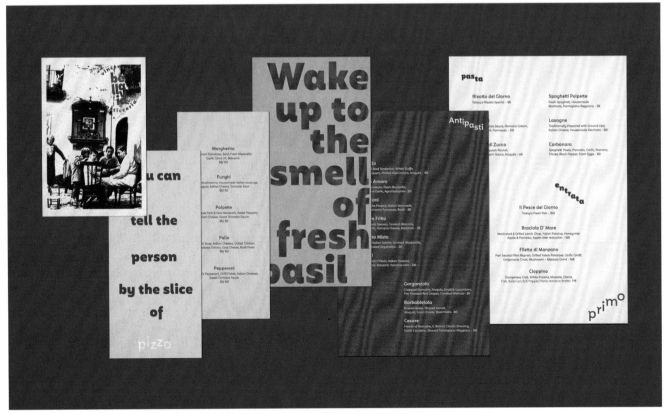

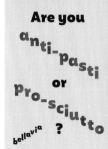

DULi

Shanghai, China

Design Agency **Pocca** | Design **Duan Zhihua**

DULi combines elements boldly from different cuisines into unique Asian inspired dishes with an emphasis on Sichuan flavour. With a vision for promoting plant-based food, DULi aims to make delicious dishes available in an accessible, casual, yet sophisticated way. Based on the consideration of the overall dining experience, without excessive visual interference, Pocca presented the restaurant's oriental moods and fusion cuisine characteristics to the diners who love the new experience of plant-based food through clear and detail-rich way and give the story to the "dining" and "food" themselves with honesty.

Durango

Durango, USA

Design Agency **meh. Design Studio**

Durango is a restaurant located in Durango, Colorado, which brings the culture of Victoria de Durango. This branding brings Mexican elements together in an unconventional graphic line. The conflict between the old and the new was displayed through posters with images of the late 19th and early 20th centuries surrounded by a more contemporary design. This project attempts to meet a balance point between different realities. The result is a combination of pop and Mexican culture elements in a single, eye-catching logo.

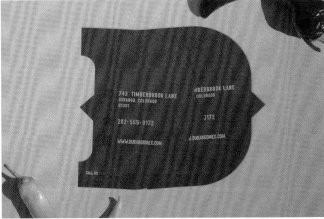

Clay Cafe & Restaurant

Penang, Malaysia

Design Agency **Where's Gut Studio** | Creative & Art Direction **Magdalene Wong**
Design **Magdalene Wong, Hee Hee** | Strategy **Focicrete**
Photography **twfreeman77, jhsonhng, Hee Hee**

As a cafe-restaurant serving an array of the clay pots and Chinese staple dishes, Clay is an imaginary sequel to the story of the on-film couple in *In the Mood for Love* by Kar-Wai Wong—Mr. Chow and Ms. Su. The design team assumed that they have a happy ending and run a clay pot restaurant in Penang with 1970s' Hong Kong style. The restaurant setting playfully blends the culture of the local coffee shops both in Penang and Hong Kong, from the menu to spatial design. The whole identity gave the on-film couple a new narrative, transformed them into a generous, out-going, and friendly neighbourhood couple.

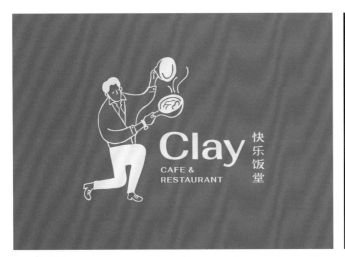

Ascari

Toronto, Canada

Design Agency & Creative Direction **Blok Design**
Client **Ascari, Erik Joyal, John Sinopoli** | Photography **Blok Design**

Erik Joyal and John Sinopoli's new Italian eatery combines their love of food and racing, paying homage to famous race car driver Alberto Ascari. Blok Design re-freshed the Ascari identity, focusing on storytelling and bringing Alberto Ascari's personality to life.

The use and layering of 1950's race car graphic language, typography, and Ascari's signature blue derived from his car add dimensionality and energy to the identity that can be felt throughout.

CON.TRO
Contemporary Bistrot

Roma, Italy

Design Agency **FUGA Studio** | Copywriting **Raffaele Notaro**
Photography **Gioia Maruccio**

CON.TRO is perceived as a sophisticated yet affordable bistrot, where people can have a slice of pizza, a gourmet dish, a custom cocktail, or a delicious haute patisserie dessert. The whole visual identity started with a few interior design renderings, with which the design team fell in love immediately—the black and white marble chevron floorings, the dark green walls, the vintage style armchairs, and touches of gold here and there. The logo and subsequent visual identity came consistently, with its geometric patterns and high contrast colours.

Camu

Miami, USA

Design Agency **Futura**

Camu is a modern Aegean food restaurant located in Miami. Aegean cuisine is the food on the islands in southern Europe, the Mediterranean Sea, and parts of Greece.

For the consumers to experience a premium and high-quality brand, Futura created a very subtle and elegant identity based on the warmth and experiences that the Mediterranean evokes in consumers.

The graphics is a series of textures that modernly reinterpret the diagrams of the balloons as well as the use of a sober colour palette that strikes for its golden details.

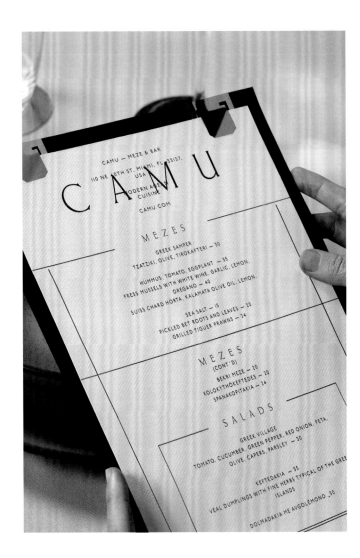

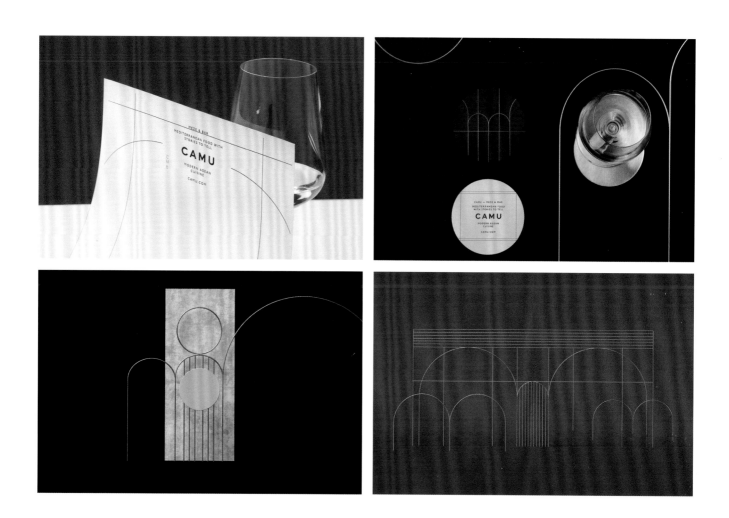

Blue Agori

Budapest, Hungary

Design Agency **David Barath Design**
Interior Design **Akos Feldman, David Barath Design**
Photography **Daniel Molnar, Solinfo, Laszlo Balkanyi**

Blue Agori wanted to stand out from its competitors from the beginning: its concept breaks with the usual Greek fast food stereotypes in gastronomy and visuality. The new design of Blue Agori is spectacular, bold, and memorable. It also includes the interior, in which simple concrete surfaces provide a perfect neutral backdrop for bright blue tiles and other identity elements.

Dopa

Sydney, Australia

Design Agency **The Colour Club** | Illustration **Andrew Yee**
Photography **Karina Lee**

The design team's direction was informed by the popular Japanese motif of transformation and the name Dopa, a shortened form of the chemical dopamine. In this case, it became an allegory for the chemically transformative experience of eating good food. During their research phase, they discovered the idiom *kishi kaisei* (wake from death, return to life), which helped inform a distinct typographic style. Since its launch, Dopa has gained a cult following and has opened a second restaurant with plans for even more soon. The merchandise has been a huge success and constantly sells out.

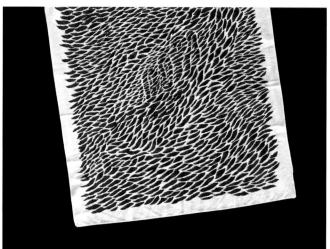

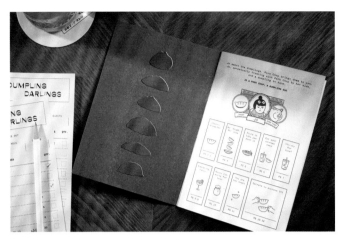

Dumpling Darlings

Singapore

Design Agency **Foreign Policy Design Group** | Creative Direction **Yah-Leng Yu** | Art Direction **Yah-Leng Yu**
Design **Fabiana Fiamnigo, Sharon Choy** | Interior Design **Elita Ong, Audrey Tan** | Illustration **Brenda Lee**

It is a dumpling bar with a twist, designed to break the mould of stereotypical Asian joints. The brand's visual language was largely inspired by the Japanese *manga* found in a *shokudo* (the casual Japanese eatery), with storylines based on the main character Jo and her pet pig, Pork Chop. The logotype was also inspired by the vertical writing system and characteristic calligraphic quality of traditional *kanji*. The contrasting mix of bright, electric colours was used to layer a pop treatment and youthful appeal to the brand. The interior design continues the visual language of a *shokudo*, translated into a casual bar with cosy lighting and tongue-in-cheek graphics in various corners. The lights and canvas at the bar counter were both inspired by the intricate folds of dumplings.

Three Uncles

London, UK

Design Agency **Studio NinetyOne** | Creative Direction **Sam Hextall**
Art Direction **Sofi Azais** | Design **Andrew Fish**
Photography **Salt Productions**

Three Uncles is a traditional Cantonese roast meat specialist. The design team created an identity that not only celebrates the main food offer, but the three founders' nostalgic memories from Hong Kong's origin. The bold logo perfectly captures the energy and repetition seen in Hong Kong's neon-clad high-rise cityscape and street culture and represents the chopping and stacking of the roasted meats. The halftone images, taken from the founders' private family archives, add nostalgia to the story. The bespoke animal icons and typography add a modern twist to this traditional Cantonese restaurant.

Milanga & Co

Buenos Aires, Argentina

Design Agency **Estudio Nuar** | Creative Direction **Melisa Rivas, Manuela Ventura, Crista Bernasconi**
Graphic Design **Crista Bernasconi, Melisa Rivas, Malena Sueiro**
Copywriting **Crista Bernasconi** | Architect & Interior Design **Pablo Chiappori Estudio**
Photography **Federico Kulekdjian, Milanga & Co**

Milanga & Co is the first fast-food restaurant in Argentina that serves only milanesa sandwiches. The design team aimed to create a brand that recalls childhood memories—a picnic flavour, a family meal, a fondness for enjoyment with closeness, and a sense of tenderness. They included elements and sayings that belong to the collective imagination of the Argentinian people.

Classic images from the heritage of those symbols were remixed into contemporary visual language. Public transports and their iconic ticket patterns, pop culture references, and daily items were combined in a nostalgia-tinged patchwork that invites people to have an old-time *sánguches*. The result is an identity that is timeless, instantly recognisable, and endearing.

Orchestra Kitchen

Madrid, Spain

Design Agency **Grávita**

Orchestra Kitchen is a new gastronomic proposal born under the dark kitchen model. Their kitchens in Madrid compose different dishes to offer a much broader experience, such as hamburgers, coquelets, tacos, and ramen.

Following the conceptual threads of music, Grávita designed a dynamic brand. Its logo with different compositions reinforces the ability to interpret different melodies (dishes). And the system was inspired by the idea of a music sheet for people to write messages that, like the notes, extend from left to right along with five-line staff.

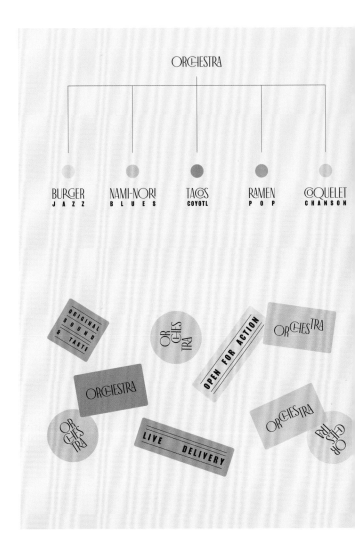

WSCHÓD BAR

Cracow, Poland

Design Agency **Studio Widok**
Design **Dawid Prząda, Paulina Suchińska**
Photography **ONI Studio**

WSCHÓD BAR is a restaurant with East Asian cuisine. "WSCHÓD" in polish means "east" as well as "sunrise." These two meanings are reflected in the logo and the whole branding. From inspiration related to Asian street food culture, neon signages, and *manga*, using bold typography and simple illustrations, the design team created a strong and consistent image of a new restaurant "rising" in Cracow's food scene.

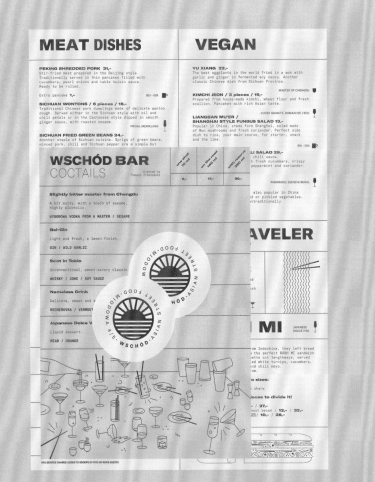
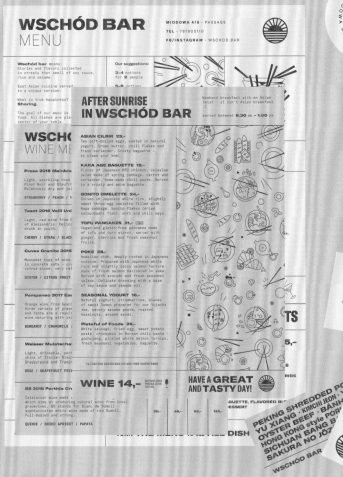

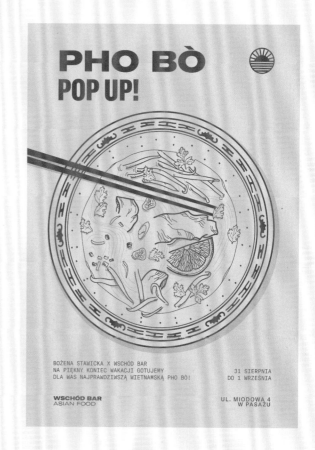

Soy

Doha, Qatar

Design Agency **Futura**

Soy is a high-end Asian *bao* restaurant located in Doha, Qatar. Soy is one of the most ancient and traditional staples found in Asian cuisine; it represents more than just an ingredient, but the basis of various Asian civilisations.

Since this ingredient takes people back to the origins and the primitive era, Futura created a graphic system where raw materials narrate the beginnings of Asian culture as people know it and where primitivism was represented with modern illustrations and graphism. Primitivism is a mode of aesthetic idealisation that recreates a primitive experience. In this case, it was represented through circles and arcs. The use of copper and rose gold creates a refined aesthetic that bridges the balance between sophistication and rawness.

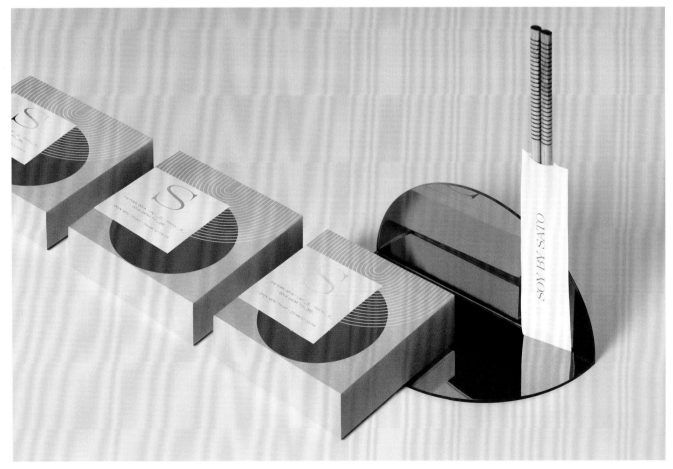

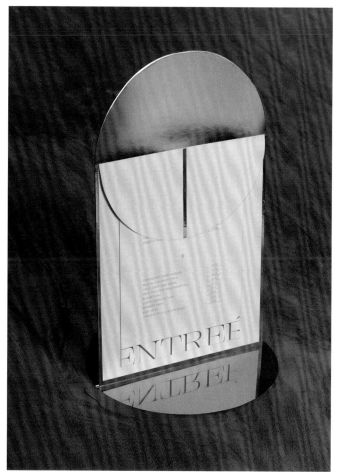

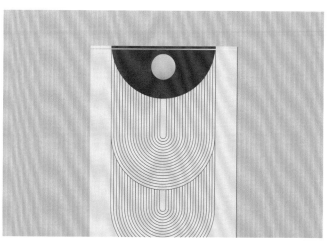

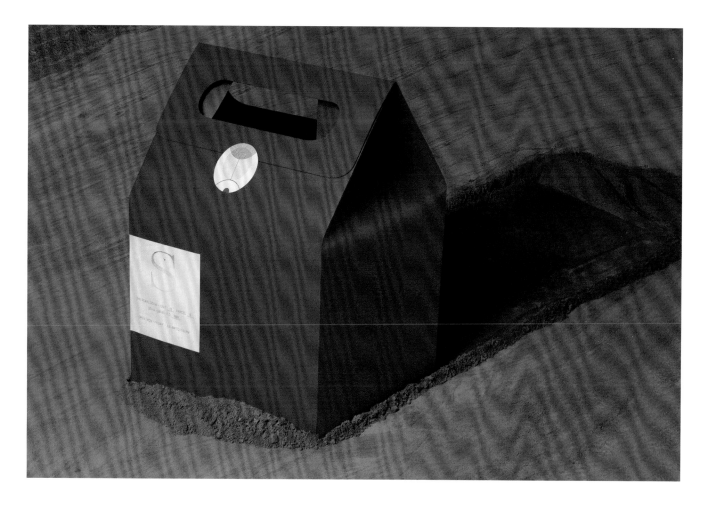

Otto!

Bratislava, Slovakia

Design Agency **NICE GUY** | Photography **Juraj Roháč**

Otto! offers typical meals of Bratislava region, influenced not only by Slovak and Czech cuisine but also by Austrian, Hungarian, and Jewish cultures. The visual identity got inspired by the visual aesthetics of restaurants and bistros in the second half of the 20th century. Hand-drew letterings, quirky typography, and simple colour palette were signature elements of many restaurants and bistros in that era. The design team's approach was to stand out from the competition but still outstand the visual aesthetics. They created an image that nicely blends in within the visuality of the city, but at the same time, the identity is strong enough to attract people not only from the city downtown.

Langos Bar

Bratislava, Slovakia

Design Agency **NICE GUY** | Architecture **Grau Architects** | Illustration **Tomáš Rybár**
Photography **Miki Curík Jr.**

Langos Bar is in the historical part of Bratislava—the Old Market Hall. So there is no shortage of people passing by. The design team wanted to use the location as the advantage, then came up with a rather unconventional and more lifestyle approach to the visual branding that is different from other businesses in that location. Langos Bar quickly caught people's attention in a couple of days and became the place to eat in the city. Instead of communicating the brand name directly, the design team decided to use a happy face as a logo. That face is easier to connect with the customers, and the face is also expressing the emotions that people can get when eating—pure happiness.

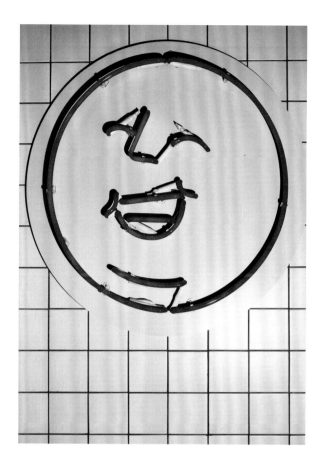

NERA

Mexico City, Mexico

Design Agency **FAENA STUDIO** | Creative Direction **Ferran Ollé**
Art Direction **Genaro Garmilla** | Production **Brenda Vergara**
Photography **Ritta Trejo**

NERA is a contemporary Italian restaurant located in Pedregal's area in Mexico City. Inspired by the surroundings and history of that area, such as rocky landscapes and residential urbanism, the designers developed a branding that workshopped an experiential concept of the restaurant. A sophisticated identity with a neutral, desaturated pallete of colours was also used in the architectural concept of the space. The special-made typography of the logotype evokes the distinctive aesthetic of the early 19th century.

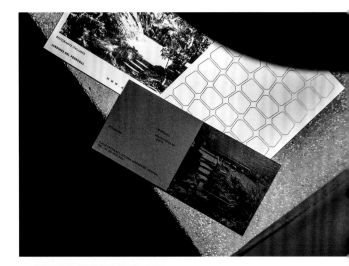

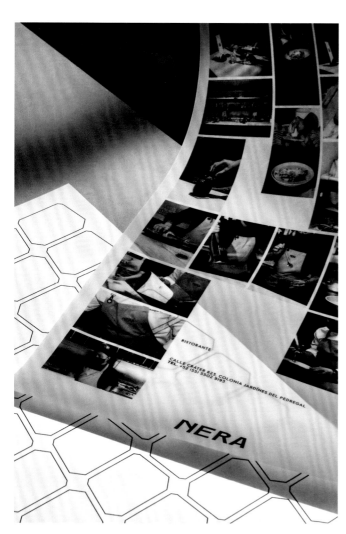

Mara

Dornoch, Scotland, UK

Design **Kieran Reilly, The Shine Agency**
Client **Links House** | Photography **Adam Lynk**

Mara's identity reflects the ethos of innovative dishes created from local, sustainable, and seasonal ingredients. A bespoke word marque was created to reflect the land and waters of the highlands in Scotland. The identity is intentionally stripped back and refined to reflect the dishes with the core ingredients. Carefully considered, tactile paper stocks and finishes across all materials add a suitably luxurious feel. Located in Dornoch, the designers took inspiration from the industrialisation of the area and Andrew Carnegie in the application of the brand utilising copper foils and Corten (weathering) steel signage situated externally and internally. The rusting of the steel over time reflects the combination of the elements and brings the character of Scotland to the plate.

Ceylon—Asian Bistro

Nizhny Novgorod, Russia

Design Agency **Kurt Studio**
Design **Jenya Shtein, Egor Shaklunov, Roman Shtein**

Ceylon asked Kurt Studio for a rebranding. To give this bistro modernity and clarity, Kurt Studio added Asian motifs in the details. In terms of the logo, Kurt Studio decided to add small notes of Asia to the Cyrillic characters. The combination of smooth lines and sharp corners helps introduce one culture into another. The colour palette was inspired by the golden glow of brass plates, green branches of palm trees, and a bright variety of spices. While working on the project, Kurt Studio tried to create a timeless solution instead of depending on visual trends. As a result, Ceylon has been successfully operating for two years, maintaining the original visual style.

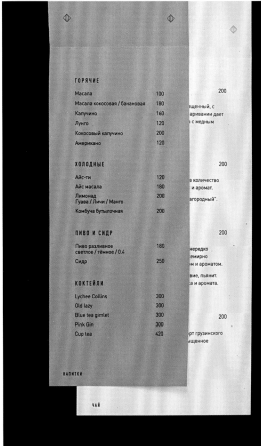

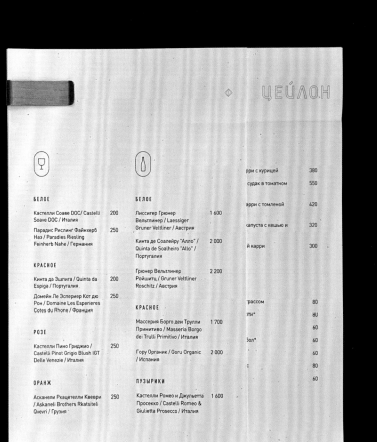

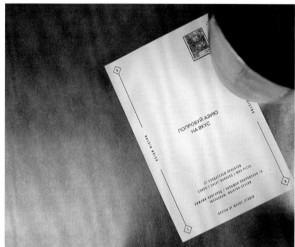

AMA

Isla Holbox, Mexico

Design Agency **Sociedad Anónima** | Photography **Juan Hernandez**

AMA is an extraordinary Japanese bar known for its respect and tradition towards recipes, products, and memorable locations on Isla Holbox near the Caribbean Sea. The design team got inspired by the long history of the *ama*—the Japanese female divers who collected oysters and pearls from the ocean. With a language attached to Japanese minimalism, illustrations, and photos, this branding project accurately represents the experience of a visit to this unique place.

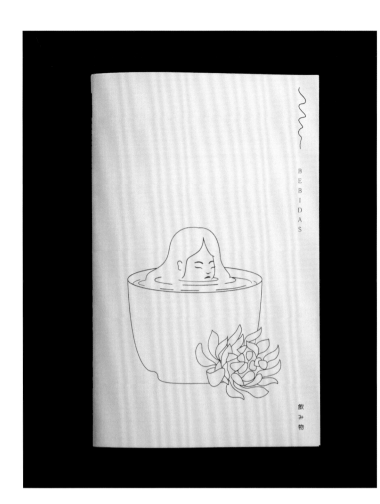

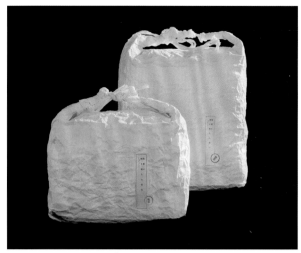

Something old, something "nou"

Barcelona, Spain

Design Agency **Studio Ingrid Picanyol**
Typography **Noe Blanco**

Bursting with ideas and energy, El Mas Vell decided to expand the restaurant's offering and present an innovative and hybrid format: restaurant, pizzeria, brewpub, and coworking place. The design team created a custom typeface inspired by the unique characteristics of Bonaventura Bassegoda's calligraphy. Bonaventura Bessegoda is the architect that built the Casino Complex of El Masnou during the years 1902–1904. Collaborating with typographer Noe Blanco, the design team developed an elegant yet dynamic typeface that pairs effortlessly and adapts seamlessly to the modular graphic system, authentic with a modernist twist.

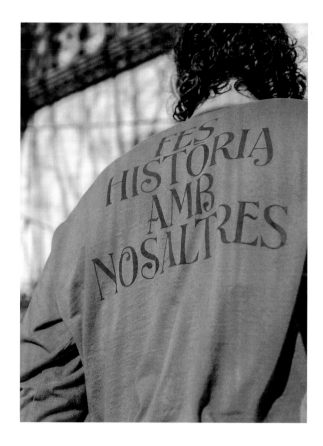

Jerome Pizzeria

Saints Petersburg, Russia

Design Agency **Sergio Laskin Agency**
Photography **Jerome Pizzeria**

Sergio Laskin Agency rebranded the design for the Jerome Pizzeria. The unique illustrations and colour combination were used to highlight the good food quality and experience. Meanwhile, the designers designed simple brand stickers for food delivery. The vibrant rebranding as the viral social media presence has made 40% client growth each month.

Sala Blanca

Guadalajara, Mexico

Design Agency **Estudio Albino**
Interior Design **Abrand & Eklemesrivial**
Client **Grupo Ambea**

Sala Blanca presents as a relaxing and natural oasis. It is an open fresh space with a feminine touch where a light kitchen reaches customers' palate accompanied by cocktails that highlight the flavours. The identity reflects this unique environment where the herons represent a light stay.

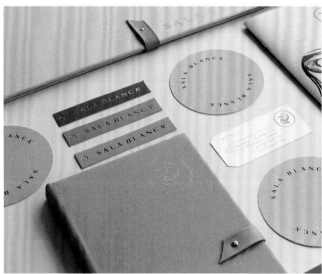

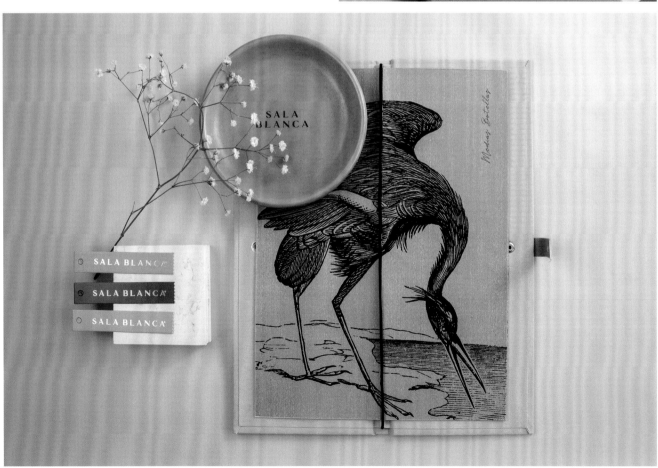

BALTA

Mexico City, Mexico

Design Agency **Sociedad Anónima** | Photography **Juan Hernandez**

BALTA is a restaurant that takes inspiration from the Mediterranean, where the fusion between European and Latin seafood cuisine can be found in a casual ambience. The design team created the brand from scratch, starting with the naming process and visual identity, all the way to its applications. The whole experience projects a classical identity and structure with a glimpse of contemporary and expressive characteristics.

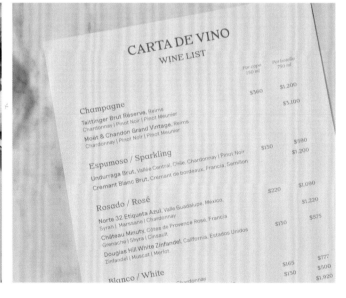

7654321

Interview with **7654321STUDIO**

7654321STUDIO, an independent creative design integration service studio, fully interprets the brand and seeks a logical way, through visual communication, using different media to convey information, allowing the brand to dialogue with consumers. As an idea creator and storyteller, 7654321STUDIO provides design consulting services for clients in various fields.

The customer group of drink shops (such as bars, milk tea shops, etc.) are mainly young people. What kind of brand design of a drink shop do you think can attract young people and enhance competitiveness?

7654321STUDIO: At present, the beverage industry on the market has a variety of styles, and there is no such a thing as industry attributes. I personally think that getting rid of the industry attributes can bring freshness to a brand, but the premise is that it can properly spread the concept of each brand while having a certain degree of visual impact and experience.

Drink shops, such as bars, are usually open at night. Do we need to pay attention to the brand design, such as whether the colour matching should consider the lighting and atmosphere of a drink shop?

7654321STUDIO: Colour and lighting atmosphere are the most intuitive feeling of a bar brand. Colours are the same as graphics and fonts. Firstly, they should be refined based on the idea and positioning of the brand to be conveyed, and then consider the issue of landing. If there is no problem, we use colour boldly in the lighting atmosphere. The consumers can feel more profound.

Why does 7654321 Studio use a lot of elements (such as boxer's portrait, slogan, and color palette of orange, blue and black, etc.) in Bar Orange? What did the client say about those elements?

7654321STUDIO: The boxer's portrait is the personal favourite of the bar owner. The slogan "corpses reviver, all die young" lets customers feel the poetry of that moment when they first come in and when they go out after drinking. The main orange colour allows consumers to have a deeper recognition and memory of the brand. The blue and black colours create a sense of mystery under the orange colour. Bar Orange is a community bar, and the owner is called "Ju Zi (Orange)." What we want to convey is to enlarge the owner's atmosphere to the details of the bar so that customers have an impression of a mysterious and poetic Japanese cocktail bar.

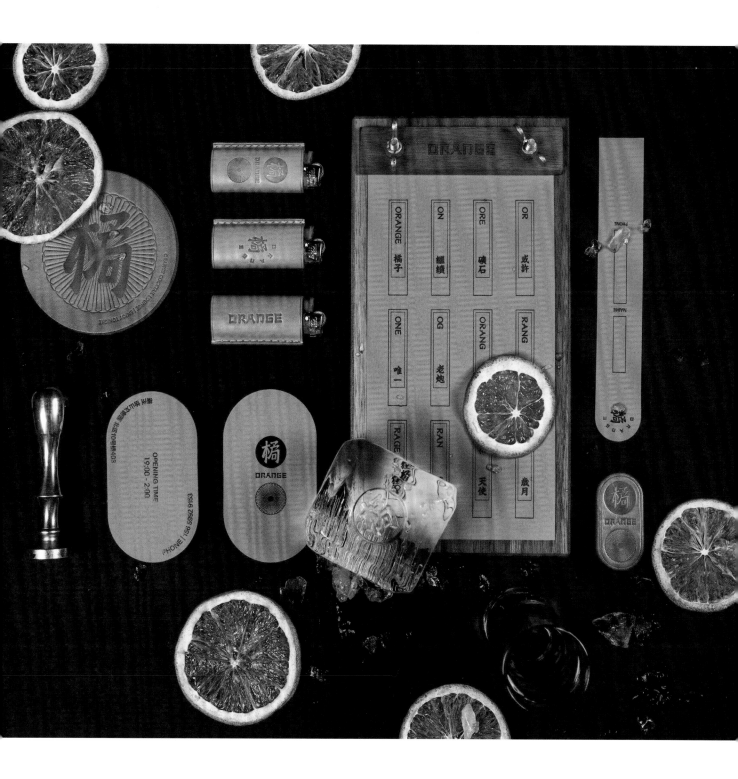

Nowadays many drink shops have become Instagram-worthy locations. Do you think this is an affirmation of the brand design of a drink shop?

7654321STUDIO: Brand design is just a small piece of content in a brand. In addition to brand design, there are many experiences and feelings generated by space, products, services, etc., which can be regarded as the completeness of the impression of a store. So mere branding is not enough.

The COVID-19 epidemic has had a significant impact on the catering industry, with drink shops bearing the brunt as a popular meeting place. In your opinion, what breakthroughs can designers seek in the brand design of drink shops?

7654321STUDIO: The epidemic has promoted online development, and online consumption habits have become more and more mature. Designers can study online language design based on online consumption methods. Online language can also be extended to offline experience, thereby creating interesting possibilities.

Bar Orange

Fuzhou, China

Design Agency **7654321STUDIO** | Design **Bosom**
Photography **Halo Xiaofang**

A photographer called Orange is a friend of the design team. He likes to share and talk with his friends. And he wanted to have his small bar to organise parties. The words "party" and "orange" are homophones in Chinese—both of them are spoken as "ju." The design team used these two homophones and combined their meaning in the design. The design team used orange, blue, and black colours as the main tones. Meanwhile, they drew an image of a boxer on the wall with the slogan "fight against yourself," which echoes the atmosphere of Orange's bar.

Fat Chow

Dubai, UAE

Design Agency **Aces of Space** | Graphics Design **Fre Lemmens (Eskader)**
Design **Andrew Theunissen, Tim Hundersmarck, Gijs Coolen**
Project Management **Babs van Hassel (Aces of Space)** | Photography **Gijs Coolen (Aces of Space)**

Fat Chow is a buzzing Cantonese restaurant and cocktail bar. The dark moody club vibe, epic neons, rough textures, and urban materials are representing the street of downtown Hong Kong. Aside from the straightforward brand identity, the designers created artwork and wall graphics, using lo-fi, goofy posters, and slogans to emphasise the urban appearance. The big neon Hakka dragon installation is almost 16 metres in length and consists of approximately 40 ribs.

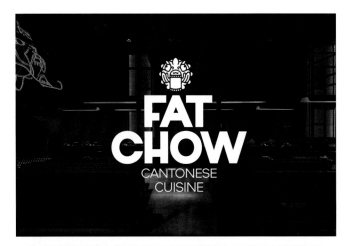

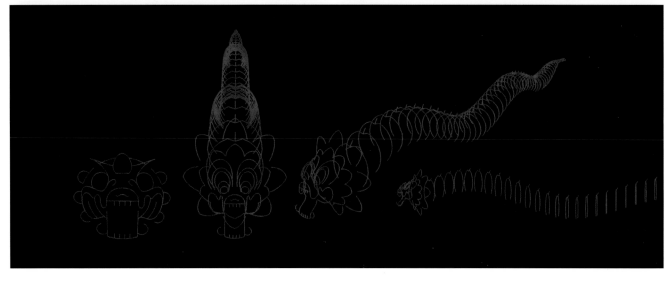

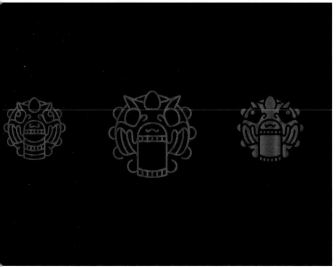

Kill Devil

Kuala Lumpur, Malaysia

Design Agency **Human** | Photography **C129 Studio**

Human rebranded the Rum Bar into something fresh and elegant, but still faithful to their traditionality. For the colour palette, Human created a high contrast between red and black to enhance the sexiness and devilish scent. Meanwhile, they developed a series of icons as a graphic language for the bar and neon signs across the interior. A modern mix of classic typefaces and provocative illustrations adds a vibrant feeling for customers. Finally, the new bar achieves and maintains an outstanding standard in food and wine, service, atmosphere and setting, which enables a reputation for gastronomy and drinks, hospitality, comfort, and exquisiteness.

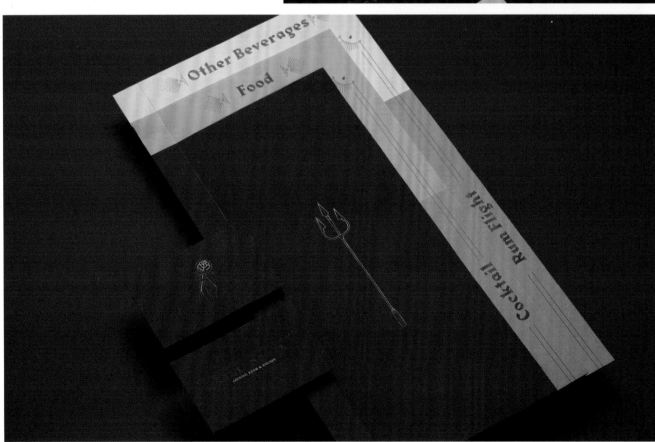

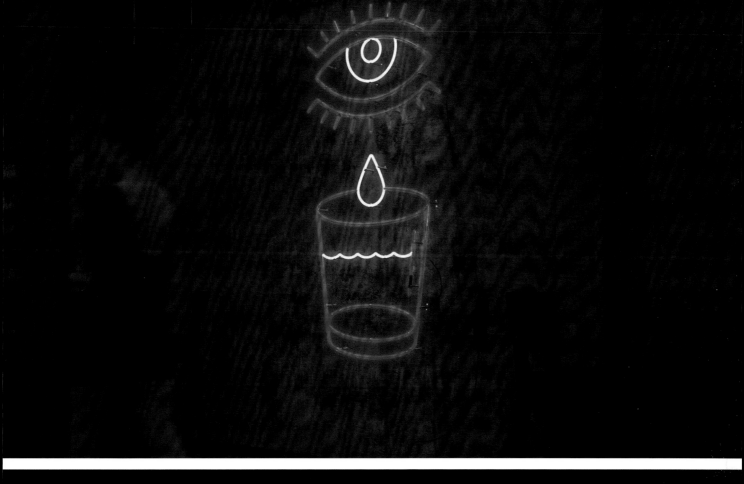

Kultura

Varna, Bulgaria

Design Agency **Marka Collective**

Kultura is a hidden bar inspired by the Prohibition period from the 1920s to 1930s in America. *Kultura* means "culture" in Bulgarian. The idea of its founders is to emphasise the hedonistic aspects of consuming cocktails. All those background details combined with the unique atmosphere. The quality drinks and the professional bartenders create one of the few distinctive places in Varna, Bulgaria. The visual blends the retro Prohibition period inspirations and a post-apocalyptic dystopian feeling together. This place brings customers back to the Prohibition period that tried to take from the people the simple pleasures in life. Kultura is an oasis for the culturals—the people who still understand the importance of transforming the random Friday night into a lifetime experience.

Kanpai!

Jakarta, Indonesia

Design Agency **Thinking Room** | Creative Direction **Eric Widjaja** | Design **Ira Carella**
Photography **Ritter Willy Putra**

Kanpai! is a Japanese-themed bar in an upscale part of Northern Jakarta. The word *kanpai* means toast in Japanese. As a brand, Kanpai! embraces the philosophy of the ability of alcohol that transcends various barriers—how people can open up and be their honest selves. There is even a slang in Japan based on this phenomenon, which is called *nomunication*. *Nomu* means "to drink" in Japanese.

This philosophy led to the selection of the creature *tanuki* as the mascot. In Japanese folklore, it is said to possess mischievous nature, and it can shape-shift to trick people. But when drunk, it couldn't hold its disguises, literally showing its true self.

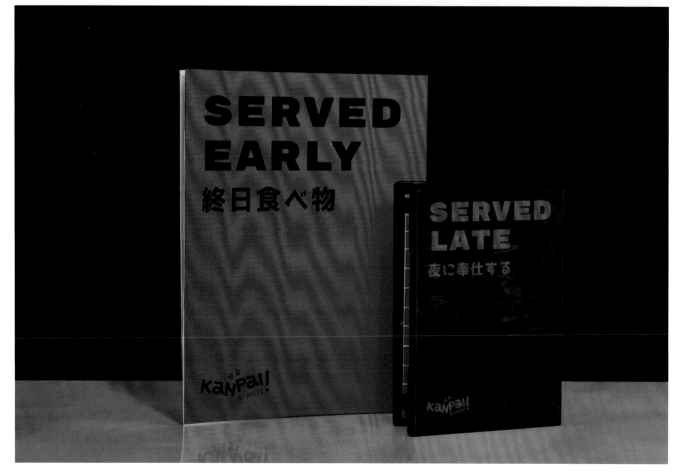

PIMS—Sexy Tea

Moscow, Russia

Design Agency **Choice Studio** | Creative Direction **Erik Musin**
Art Direction **Aleksey Zadorozhny**
Design **Elena Astakhova (Identity)**, **Timofey Popandopulo (Visualisation)**

PIMS is a tea-based drink with different flavours. It is a new place and a new community where no one is afraid to be themselves and do what they want. PIMS is not just tea but a drink that can interact with customers' mood and taste. As a result, PIMS has become a real trendsetter for the masses.

Niou Tea

Taipei, Taiwan, China

Design Agency **Odd Institute** | Creative Direction **Van Chen** | Design **Alien Wu**

Niou Tea is a fashionable fusion of ancient Chinese prescriptions and contemporary trendy drinks. The visual identity is based on "clash and contest" and extends concepts such as "life is a struggle" and "win-win is so boring." The panther symbolises the spirit of unyielding and creates a unique beverage brand based on metal materials. The whole brand has cleverly caught up with the fitness craze in recent years, becoming a popular drink in the fitness field. Besides, within half a year of opening, it was invited to open a pop-up store in Osaka, Japan, and it is also very popular.

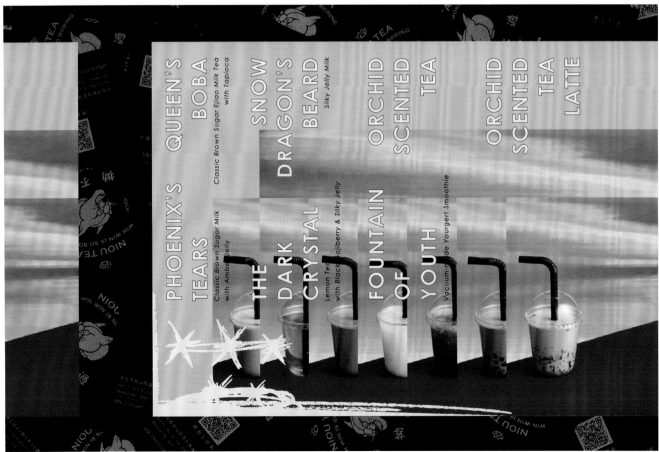

Deck Taproom

Xiamen, China

Design Agency **Atelier NOA** | Design Direction **Zhu Hua**
Design **Yin Zishuo** | Client **NOA Hotel**

Deck Taproom is a small integrated business space, which can be treated as a cafe, bar, office, or social gathering. Inspired by the idea of a cabin, the design is based on the top view of the hull that summarises the space in full. It uses the way of the sketch to exhibit the handcrafted sense of granule, in order to form the logo. The design of the visual identity also benefits from the slenderness and overlap of the space.

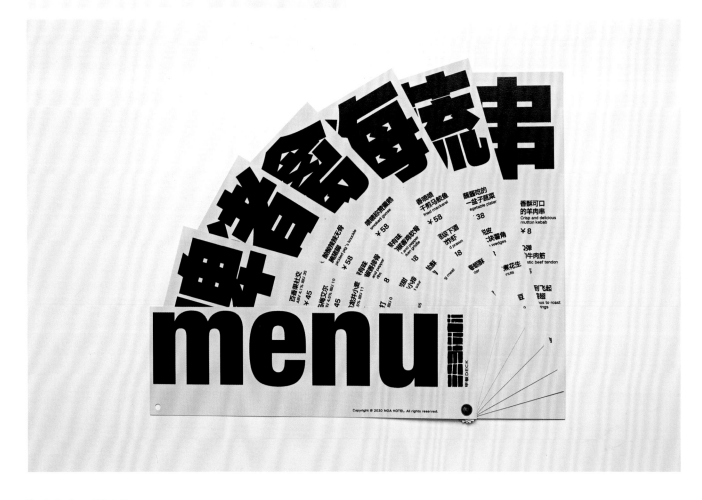

BOBA
Bubble Tea & Food

Milan, Italy

Design **Elisabetta Vedovato, Lorenzo Mercanti**

The designers were asked to create an identity for a small cafe in Milan to reinvent the classic bubble tea shop. This new concept brings together the authentic bubble tea from Taiwan, China, with genuine street food from different cultures. The polar bear hugging on a tapioca sphere represents the dream and characteristics of the owner. Now the cafe is a familiar and relaxing place, suitable for families and young people.

Nación Brava

Mérida, México

Design Agency **Mantra** | Creative Direction **Rodrigo Guillermo**
Graphic Design **Braulio Campos**
Set Design **Daniel Avila** | Photography **Elías Avilez, Elías Collí**

Nación Brava is a craft beer bar that offers authentic taste experiences in a warm and accessible atmosphere. Mantra created the brand inspired by the sense of belonging and designed it by hand, then digitised it later to preserve the small imperfections that arose in the process, thus capturing the artisan touch that characterises Nación Brava's beer. For the colour palette, Mantra started with one of the elements that represent the brand's characteristic—bravery. Mantra maintained neutrality with black and white backgrounds, adding loud touches of colour in vibrant red and yellow-brown.

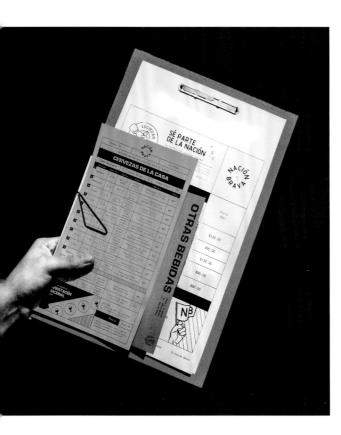

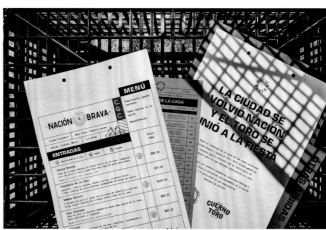

Santo Secreto

Yucatán, Mexico

Design Agency **Puro Diseño**

Legend has it that in Calzada del Fraile, the most emblematic street in Valladolid, Yucatán. There is an old secret passage, where the friars, tired of monotony, hid to think, hang out, drink, laugh, dance, and above all to share their most intimate secrets. Over time, this place was abandoned. And the vegetation buried the passage.
Santo Secreto is a magical place that echoes Calzada del Fraile's legend. A space that mixes tradition and innovation to create a destination of experiences for its visitors.

PIPNDROP

Moscow, Russia

Design Agency **Suprematika** | Creative Direction **Vladimir Lifanov**
Design **Alena Shulga** | Project management **Maria Kazakevich**

PIPNDROP is a wine bar with an author's cuisine. It is located in the business park Tovarischestvo Ryabovskoy Manufactury, a creative cluster in Moscow. The bar is named after fictional wine ghosts—pipndrops that live in empty bottles. And sometimes bar visitors can see them in the middle of the party in a reflection of a wine glass. Pipndrops are always in high spirits and this is fully reflected in the identity of the bar.

WILD LEGS

Moscow, Russia

Design **Astakhova Elena**

WILD LEGS is a modern bar. People can pair the wine with a selection of fish and seafood, meat, poultry, or snacks and desserts. WILD LEGS has achieved beauty in simplicity as an art form. If the customer twists the wine in the glass, it will hit the wall and begin to roll down. This effect is not only in the naming but also in the customised font and illustrations. WILD LEGS creates an atmosphere for bringing people together. The brand is playful and recognisable and can grow and scale further because food and wine speak for themselves.

wine

(wine legs)

+

food

(fish and seafoods/
meat / poultry)

=

wild legs

(wine and food)

2F Beer Garden

Ho Chi Minh City, Vietnam

Design Agency **M — N Associates** | Design **Duy — N**
Project Management **M — Lan**
Photography **Deto Concept, Hau Le**

The brand name 2F originally comes from the address of the eating place, 2F Nguyễn Thành Ỷ. The visual identity is all about beer, always casual and fun. The system was based on the psychology of beer lovers. They can be enjoyable to have fun and make friends easier. With the rebranding, 2F represents a new sustainable and fun identity to be recognised in the downtown. Meanwhile, the *quán* concept (small houses built in the middle of the field to avoid rain and sun) makes customers enjoy without being dominated by heavily graphic decoration.

always casual   always fun

2F DOWNTOWN BEER

Jigger Cocktail & Wine Bar

Hanoi, Vietnam

Design Agency **Cohe Studio**
Design **Hoang Hiep, Le Qui Ta**
Photography **Quang Tung**

To avoid the cliché of ordinary drink shops, Cohe Studio created a unique visual identity for the Jigger Cocktail & Wine Bar. Everything there is great, from an eclectic selection of music, vibrant atmosphere to the superb mixology experience. Cohe Studio got inspiration from the roaring 1920s of the American dream, such as jazz music, the concept of alcohol prohibition, and the Art Deco Movement.

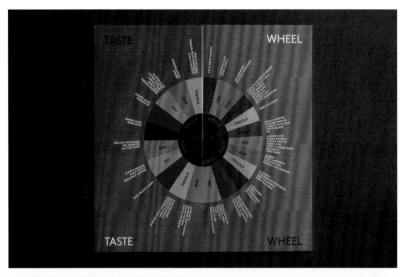

NOLA Kitchen

Porto, Portugal

Creative Direction **Carla Almeida**
Design **Bernardo Braga**

The design team wanted to make NOLA Kitchen synonymous with simplicity. They created a minimal identity that is as pure as NOLA Kitchen's recipes. Appraised by locals as simple and healthy and featured in numerous magazines and city guides as the new trendy spot, NOLA Kitchen is a reference of simple modern food in Porto.

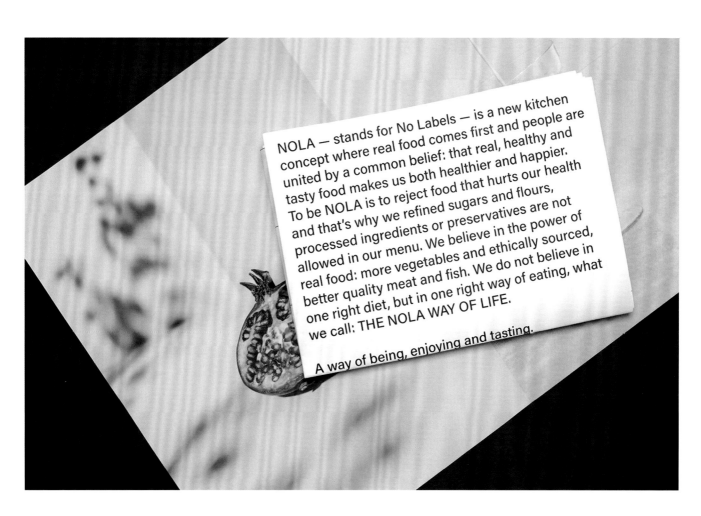

NOLA — stands for No Labels — is a new kitchen concept where real food comes first and people are united by a common belief: that real, healthy and tasty food makes us both healthier and happier. To be NOLA is to reject food that hurts our health and that's why we refined sugars and flours, processed ingredients or preservatives are not allowed in our menu. We believe in the power of real food: more vegetables and ethically sourced, better quality meat and fish. We do not believe in one right diet, but in one right way of eating, what we call: THE NOLA WAY OF LIFE.

A way of being, enjoying and tasting.

Coup de Tête

Paris, France

Art Direction & Design **Néstor Bada** | Client **Coup de Tête**
Photography **Néstor Bada**

In French, *Coup de Tête* has three meanings: a head-butt, a moment of the spur, and a well-known French film in 1979. The visual identity is a result of all three ideas above. Inspired by the French Novuelle Vague, the logo revolves around a hand-drawn and playful hand cheering glass of wine. Customised typography evolves to be adapted to different sizes and formats, and everything is highlighted by little touches of abstract shapes that represent the spontaneous spirit of Coup de Tête.

Appendix – Coffee & Bar

Hong Kong, China

Design Agency **StudioWMW** | Creative & Art Direction **Sunny Wong**
Design **Kylie Lee**

The design idea generated from the name of appendix. It promotes slow living and culture in the day time, while a leisure bar at night. The appendix also refers to the end section of the book. Thus, a flexible identity is born.

Inspired by its flexibility, the design team transformed the concept into a paperclip with a hidden initial "a" to form the core logo and further extend to collateral development. For example, the menu sheets held together with a paperclip. This concept does not only expand the visual language, but allow the appendix to mix and match different menu sheets for different scenarios.

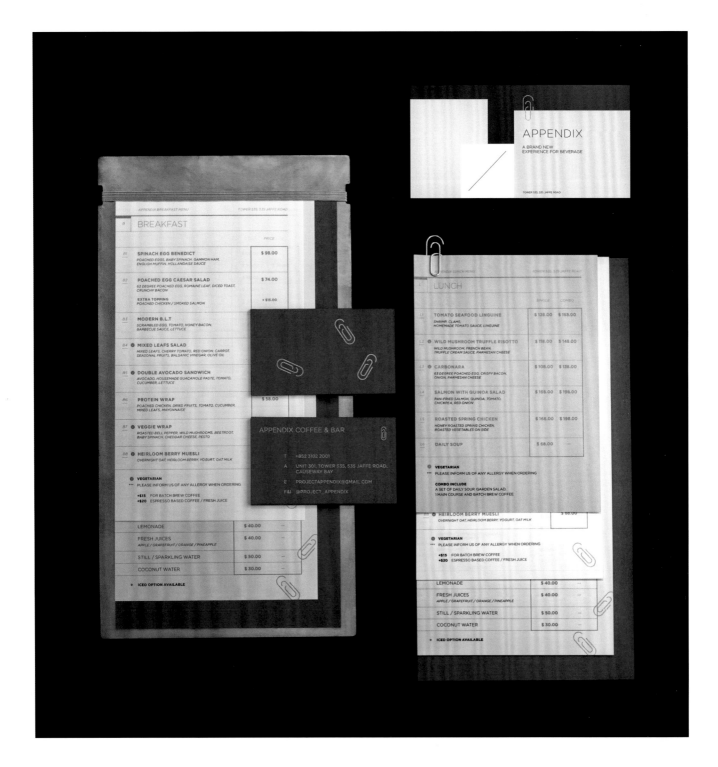

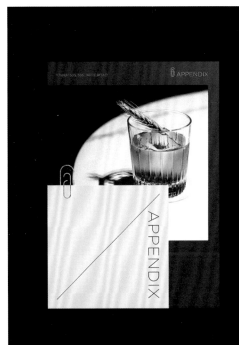

Cocó

Acapulco, Mexico

Design **Ana Patron Toffano**

Cocó is a branding identity for a seafood restaurant and cocktail bar. It was inspired by the golden age of Acapulco, Mexico's forsaken paradise. The construction of Art Deco hotels was in full flow in Acapulco from the 1940s to 1970s, which created a golden age.

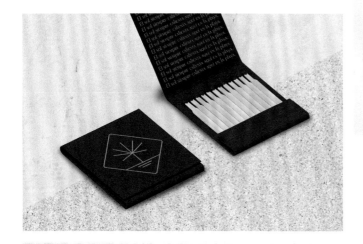

Dessert
Shops &
Bakeries

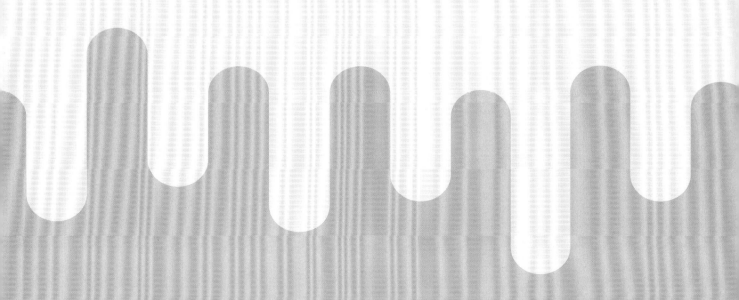

The Lab Saigon is a company of creative professionals in strategy, identity, spatial design, communication, and emerging media.

Interview with **The Lab Saigon**

The dessert shops and bakeries have always been favoured by young people. What graphic design elements do you think can attract their attention?

The Lab Saigon: The subtle surprises and little stories are created for young people to discover. The trendy eating places with vivid visuals often attract Instagrammers. But to attract and keep their attention, we need to allow for authentic discovery. We use illustrations to bring humour into space. For example, instead of a WC signage, we drew a person sitting on the toilet and using a phone. We don't talk about this graphic design element at all. It's just there for the audience to discover. It tells the customers that we are honest and understand them, but we don't take ourselves too seriously. Designers should design subtle moments like this.

Which one is more important, the taste and quality or the branding of a bakery?

The Lab Saigon: Taste and quality, but branded. Otherwise, nobody knows about your great taste and quality.

The dessert shops and bakeries pay attention to the sweet and harmonious space atmosphere. What do you think should be paid attention to in colour matching and graphic design? Can you talk about it with your Bakes Flagship project?

The Lab Saigon: There are two general strategies. Your spatial and graphic design can complement each other, or they can contrast each other. We use both. Our daily products are designed to be complementary to space's atmosphere. We use raw materials and neutral colours to pack our daily products, which sits harmoniously with the natural stone in the spatial design. For our special occasion products, we use colours that contrast the space to draw attention.

Many dessert shops and bakeries have become Instagram-worthy locations. Do you think they are affirmations of their brand design?

The Lab Saigon: We think great brand design helps a business become part of the target audience's life. Instagram and Pinterest have their role in getting the word out there, but it's short-lived. Brand design should sustain interest in the business beyond the initial hype.

In the background of the COVID-19 epidemic, the food delivery industry is booming. What new challenges bring to the dessert shops and bakeries' brand design?

The Lab Saigon: Nowadays, fancy restaurants are not able to rely on plain takeout boxes anymore. The delivery packaging system becomes extremely important in three areas: sustainability, hygiene, and customer experience. They reduce not only waste but also the spread of viruses and bacteria. Meanwhile, they can maintain a level of customer experience that the customers expect the brand to have.

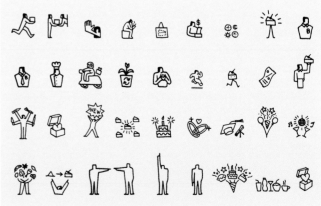

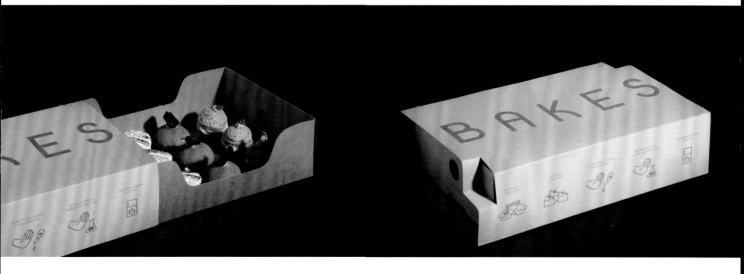

Bakes Flagship

Ho Chi Minh City, Vietnam

Design Agency **The Lab Saigon** | Creative Direction **Tuan Le**
Graphic Design **Trang Dinh, Tran N Nguyen, Jay Vu**
Strategy **Ly Tong, Tuan Dao** | Illustration **Reo Le**
Photography **Do Sy, Thuy Truc, Kai Nguyen, Duong Gia Hieu**

Bakes Flagship is a French patisserie that believes pastry should be like love: simple, thoughtful, and honest. The Lab Saigon designed a brand with nothing to hide, an honest identity inside out, from packaging to architecture. Wordmark crafted from Bakes Sans, The Lab Saigon's bespoke font in one confident weight, balancing curves, straight edges, and mostly monospaced glyphs, for a clean but friendly vibe.

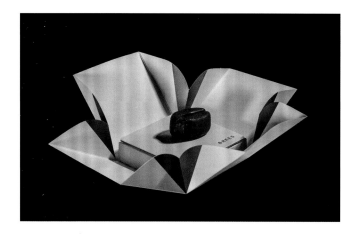

Mòlt. Bakery

València, Spain

Design Agency **democràcia estudi** | Design **Javi Tortosa, Migue Martí**

Making bread is easy, but making it different and putting a differential stamp on it is a more complex task. Mòlt is clear about its target audience and required better visibility. To be able to transmit Mòlt's value, the designers came up with a new image—a movement of a wheat grain mill. The fluorescent red colour of the brand represents the fire and the grey colour of the flour. The new branding has become a graphic translation of good-quality local bread and zero-waste. Meanwhile, the designers created a nice wrapper for the takeaway. They thought that a good meal should not be limited to beautiful plates, but can be enjoyed anytime, anywhere.

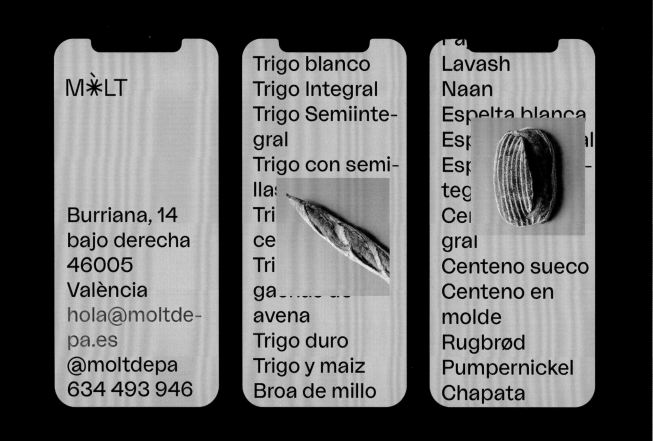

Scoop

San Pedro Garza García, Mexico

Design Agency **Parámetro Studio** | Photography **Agencia Blanca**

Parámetro Studio designed Scoop, a casual yoghurt, coffee, and milkshakes shop located in the heart of San Pedro Garza García. Scoop is a place to experience a softening vibe to grab an ice cream in the summer and coffee in the winter. The interior features a design full of natural light and funny surfaces, pink and mint green seating, white and black floors, cream walls, and

gold details. They are part of the vintage and cosy chic vibe. The designers created the logo with custom-scripted typography. The graphic identity centres on different types of typography, hand-made labellings, and carefully-selected messages on every single package, deliverable, and sign.

Yaourti

Montreal, Canada

Design Agency **Tux Creative Co** | Creative Direction **Charlene Sepentzis**
Graphic Design **Joanie Brisebois** | Copywriting **Élyse Noël de Tilly**

With one of the highest rates of restaurants per capita in North America, Montreal is known for its culinary diversity and creativity. Tux needed to design a unique, credible, and inviting experience for Yaourti in an extremely dynamic and competitive landscape. By reinterpreting some key aspects, such as the iconic ancient arches and certain Hellenic forms, Tux created a graphic language that is undeniably Greek in appearance but brimming with modernity.

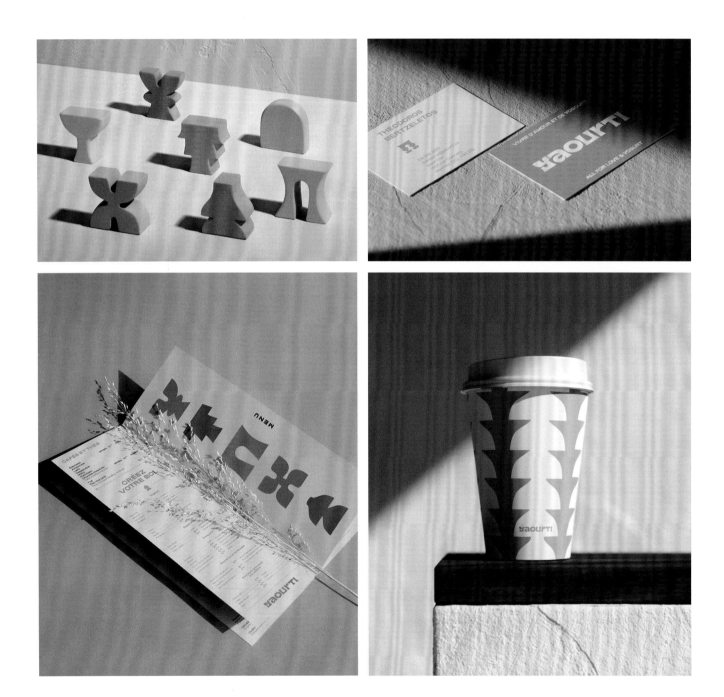

KeungKeung

Seoul, South Korea

Design Agency **Studio IeM** | Design **Minseong Jeon** | Consulting **Seungyong Sun**

KeungKeung, which means Sniff, Sniff, is a sound of getting the smell of freshly baked goods. The smell is one of the strongest senses that has a magical power to attract people's instincts. The logotype was developed based on the shape of the word with the use of bright yellow colour. The design team utilised the geometric elements—lines and circles—of the character. And even for those who do not know how to read Korean, the geometric logotype looks harmonious and consistent with the overall layout.

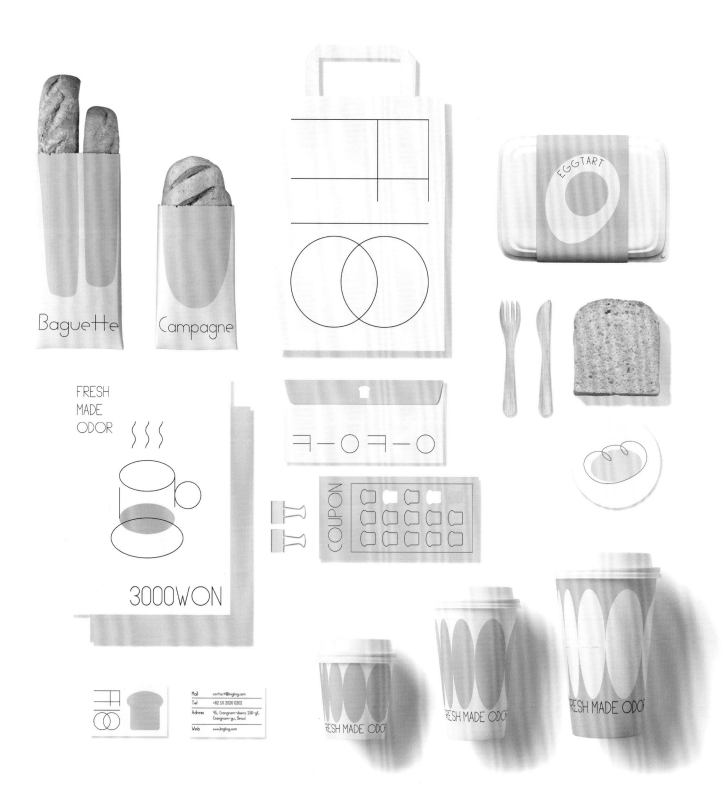

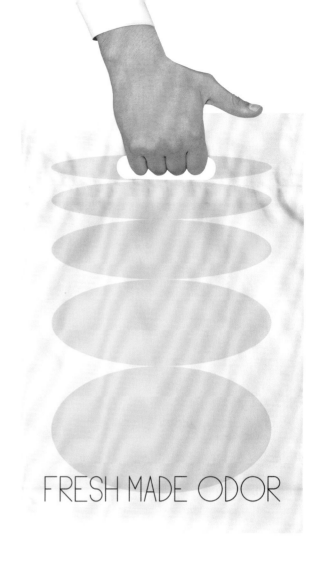

FRESH MADE ODOR

di Pâle

Córdoba, Argentina

Design Agency **Estudio Nuar** | Design **Melisa Rivas, Manuela Ventura**
Architect **Gruppo Arquitectos**

di Pâle offers a different approach from the other ice-cream stores in Córdoba. It provides a combination of two classics: the authentic Italian gelateria and the delicate French patisserie. The task of the design team was to create a fresh and delicate brand that can go beyond the limits of a traditional creamery without losing the Italian style. With this premise, they did naming, brand's images, architecture applications, and prints. They used pastel colours and a combination of classic typographies to create a warm and harmonic ambience. They proposed a simple yet friendly photographic mood to highlight homemade values.

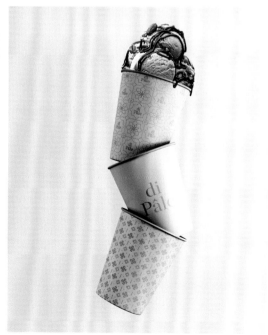

Eisperle

Graz, Austria

Design Agency, Creative & Art Direction **Bruch—Idee & Form**
Interior Design **Perz+Gartler**
Photography **Stiefkind (Interior), Lena Kinast (Food)**

The ice cream is melting in the sun. Various tastes flow into each other while creating new and fascinating shapes and colour combinations. With this feeling in mind, the designers decided to create a new corporate design concept for the first pure vegan ice cream shop in Graz called Die Eisperle. The versatile forms and colour combinations vary on every touchpoint and communicate a summerly attitude to life. They show a creative and adventurous approach to Die Eisperle's curious ice cream varieties. The signets display the personal ice cream moment and can be adapted to any personality type—because ice cream is something for everyone.

PLOUF

Seoul, South Korea

Design Agency **Studio IeM** | Art Direction & Illustration **Catherine Potvin**
Graphic Design **Simon Langlois**
App Design **Minseong Jeon** | Coordination **Jieun Kwak**

The design team designed the overall visual and applications of PLOUF, using the brand emblem developed by Catherine Potvin's characters' illustrations and Simon Langlois's logotype. The drawing touch of the main characters and the witty san serif logotype are used as a signature. They set blue and ivory as the main colours and pink and orange-red as sub-colours, which are applied to the various components. They believe that brands with authentic stories attract people. And they also did a better job of building a personal relationship with each customer. As they expected, the posters of PLOUF characters and dessert kits got the most attention from the audience, and they had an impact on the brand's sales.

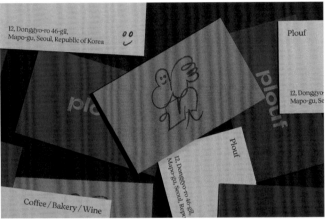

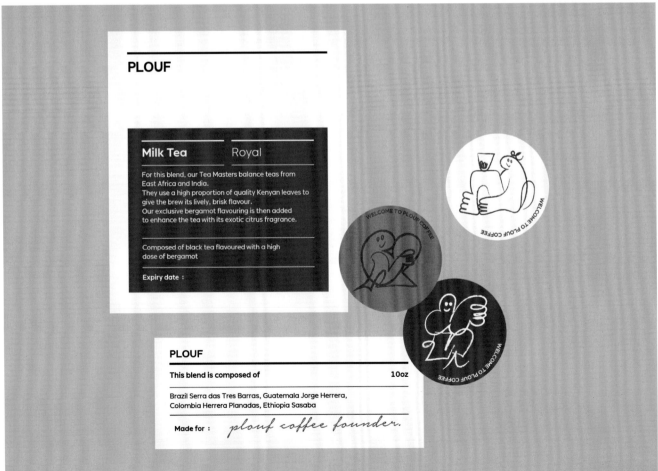

NOTICE DESSERT

It is recommended to eat within 2 days of purchase, and it can be stored in the freezer until 30 days.

Mélimélo Bakery

Zapopan, Mexico

Design **Daniela Arcila**

Mélimélo is a lovely Mexican and French fusion pastry shop. Its name in French means "combination" or "mix of two things." Mélimélo's identity with geometric patterns was inspired by the most famous Mexican and French bread, *Pan de Muerto* and *baguettes*. The blatant logo variation on the business cards represents the vibrance, carefree, and embodiment of the Mexican spirit that throws traditional conventions to the wind.

The bright colours with brushes of light pink and gold are complemented by a sweet and contemporary touch. Daniela Arcila took this project on as a challenge of creating a brand that can combine two completely different countries in a clean, subtle, and simple way.

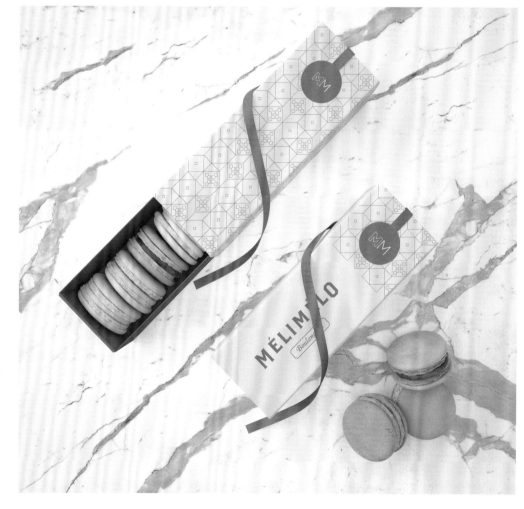

Messer Bakery

Medellín, Colombia

Art Direction **Tats Oquendo**
Design **Tats Oquendo, Tavo Gómez**

Messer Bakery is a family brand of women entrepreneurs. In this project, two designers wanted the brand to reflect the warmth Messer Bakery always offers to its customers and love for good cuisine. Two designers felt that Messer Bakery was like a small home where everyone felt part of the family, so they decided to represent handmade style illustrations without losing good taste. And they designed the logo that would go in a typographic style that displays femininity and elegance with a mix of vintage and contemporary style.

EL BALANCE

ENTRE

AMOR & SABOR

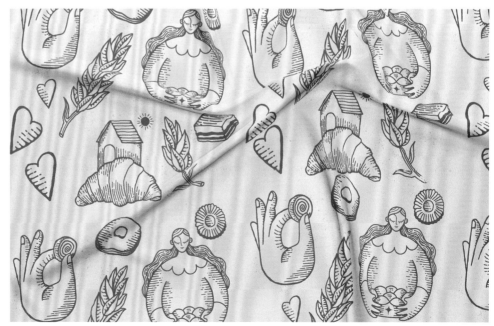

Melted

Denver, USA

Design Agency **Wunder Werkz** | Client **HECH**

Wunder Werkz's mission for Melted was to make ice cream sexy, edgy, and funny. They started with creating a brand ethnography followed by naming and brand positioning. Their goal was to make the logomark as tasty as ice cream, from a distinctive, disconnected drip of the M to the easy flowing curves and elongated counters throughout the letterforms. The soft logomark, paired with a semi-ribald illustration system, avoids clichés and excites a new narrative: ice cream can be sexy too. With the diverse illustrative system, they created sticker packs for customers to take the liberty of branding their cups of ice cream. They also rolled out a wheatpaste campaign that covers the interior and exterior brick walls of the space.

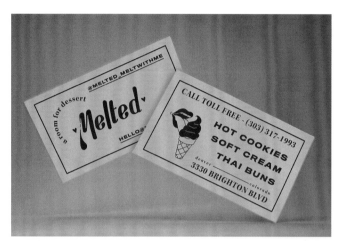

P1

Paris, France

Design Agency **Brand Brothers**

P1 is an organic artisanal bakery and bakery workshop where people learn to make their own bread. The founder entrusted Brand Brothers with the design of P1's visual identity. Their response was based on an architectural monogram, with very contrasting lines, associated with a monospaced, elegant, and technical typeface, as well as a few natural coloured spots. The set allows the space to be wrapped discreetly and sharply, leaving the emphasis on materials and products; a right dose of graphic design, such as punctuation, expresses the state of mind that guides the creation of this new kind of bakery.

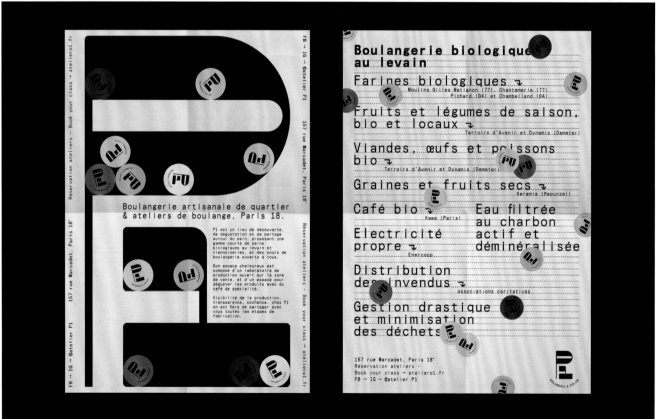

Nancy

Santo Domingo, Dominican Republic

Art Direction, Design & Copywriting **Tiare Hernández Payano** | Copy Editing **Katherine Lorenzo**
Food Photography **Denis Karpenkov, Natasha Breen** | Illustration **Studio Graphic Goods**

Nancy is a family-owned pastry and cafe with over 21 years of unique experience in the market. The graphic solution alluded to the current gastronomic proposal rich in Caribbean elements and unparalleled impressions. A neutral colour palette was applied, supported with a photographic style inspired by the Spanish still life of the 17–18th centuries and typography that maintains its readability. They gave the brand a sense of the font Nitti-like discretion and the fonts Cirka and Delova-liked grace. Meanwhile, the exquisite vintage botanical illustrations of Pierre-Joseph Redouté play an important role of communication intermediate.

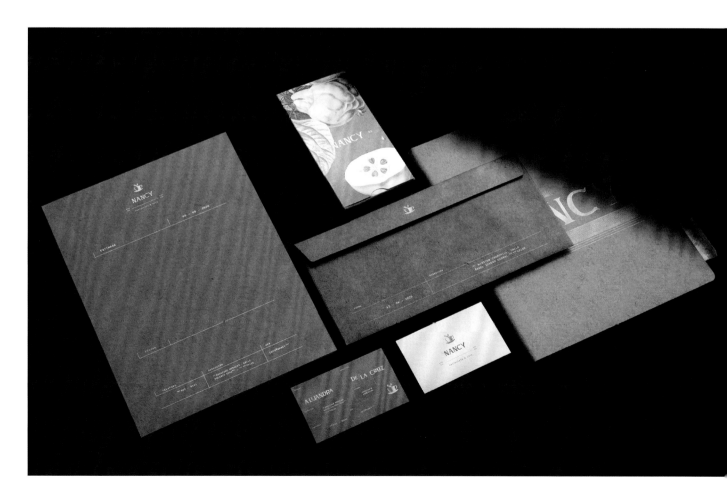

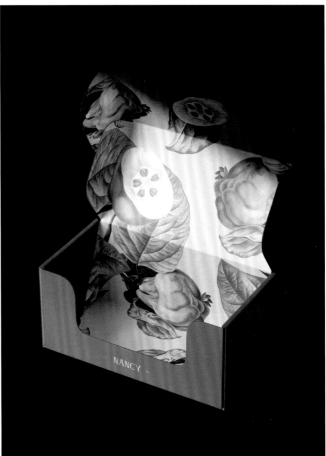

Jungle Coffee

Samara, Russia

Design Agency **HeyMoon Agency** | Art Direction **Natasha Nikulina**
Illustration **Petr Naumov**
Photography **Olesya Shi (Interior), HeyMoon Agency (Branding)**

Jungle Coffee sells sweet bagels and donuts with tropic coffee in the centre of the old Samara town. The designers focused on Jungle Coffee's graphic and packaging design to attract the customers, such as the donut box with jungle leaves illustration, takeaway cups with sloth mascot. Meanwhile, the packaging is not only inexpensive and convenient for an employee to assemble, but also echos the interior and brand design of Jungle Coffee.

Dora

Porto Alegre, Brazil

Design Agency **Abio Design**
Design **Eduardo Vicente da Silveira, Lara Rei, Matheus Marques, Vitoria Collato, Lucas Franca**
Photography **Matheus Marques**

Dora is a wild fermentation bakery, a place where everything revolves around bread. All the side dishes, drinks, coffee, and wine can harmonise with the bread. The challenge was to develop a manifesto that would convey the business value proposition and design a flexible visual identity rich in details that had an irreverent character.

Juju

Singapore

Design Agency **Fable**

Nestled in the heart of Botanic Gardens, a UNESCO heritage site, Juju serves up healthy smoothies, juju bowls, sandwiches, slow-pressed juice, coffee, brewed tea, and more.

This prismatic and upbeat identity got inspired by The Memphis Group, which features diverse patterns and abstract aesthetics. The colour family is mainly pastel interspersed with darker analogous tones, depending on usages and placements physically and digitally. The illustrations and graphic applications were executed across various touch-points to represent Juju's personality—empathetic, upbeat, and appreciation of life.

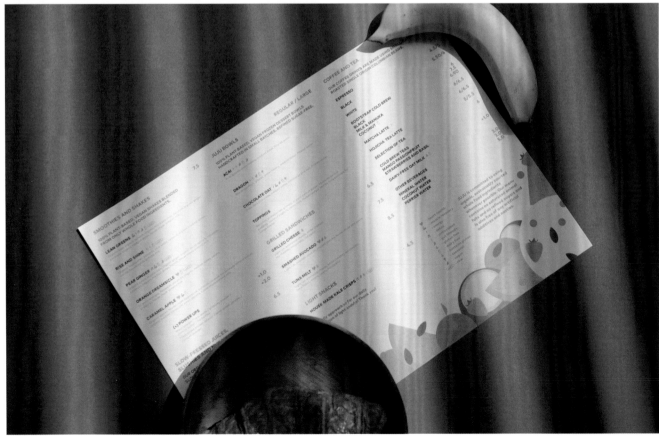

Holiland Lab

Shanghai, China

Design Agency **cheeer STUDIO**

Holiland Lab is an offline conceptual store owned by Holiland, a Chinese bakery brand. It is located in THE HUB, Shanghai. The design team utilised experimental design to show the new concept of bakery, including the visual identity, fonts, and graphics.

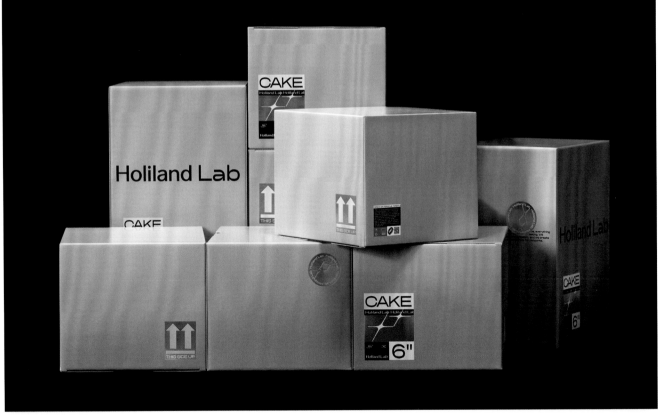

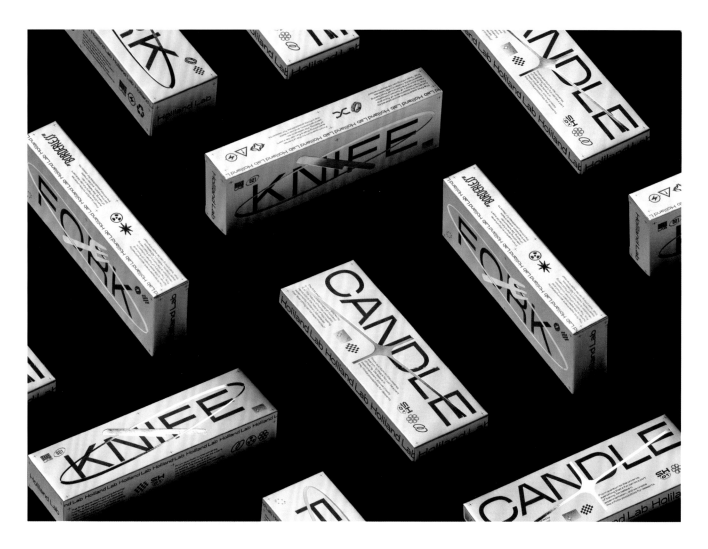

Napa

Melbourne, Australia

Design Agency **Both** | Design **Sigiriya Brown, Dan Smith**
Photography **Shelley Horan**

Both was engaged to create an identity for Napa, a new eatery positioned in a bustling part of Glen Iris, Victoria. Steering away from any obvious visual tropes associated with the venture's namesake, the Napa Valley in California, Both focused on the experiential qualities of that region: the sense of space, the rich soils, and the wide-open blue sky. The resulting design revolves around an understated and uncluttered visual language underpinned by a textural palette to reflect the warmth and relaxed pace of the Napa Valley. Meanwhile, Both created the signage which helps Napa stand out from the neighbouring shops.

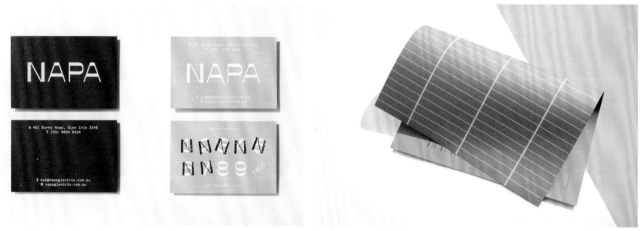

Folio Q8
Bakery Branding

Kuwait City, Kuwait

Design Agency **H3I Branding Agency**
Photography **UNSPLASH**

An interior designer called Mariam asked the design team to create her own bakery's brand. The project focuses on Mariam's personal preferences and characteristics, such as cats, *folie* (creaziness in French), and Q8 (the abbreviation of Kuwait).

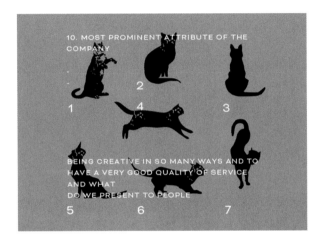

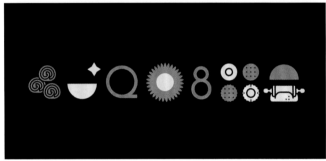

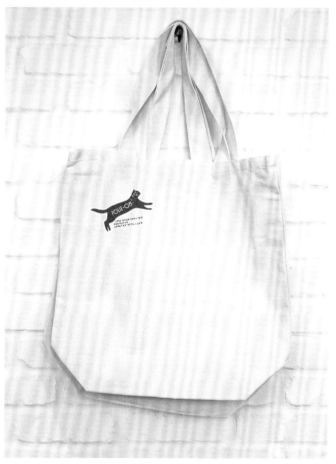

Felicidad Bakery

Medellín, Colombia

Design Agency **invade** | Art Direction **Laura Hoyos**
Photography **invade**

Felicidad is a bakery that offers cookies and ready-to-bake cookie doughs. They want to sell their products with a simple yet strong message: happiness is for everyone. The recipe for the creative process combined a pinch of nostalgia, lots of primary colours, and some memories of the bakery from childhood. As a result, Felicidad's brand identity is contagious, just like happiness. Felicidad's character was called Felizpe. His particular tone of voice and distinctive yellow colour has been translated to all touchpoints. That has become a very recognisable brand anywhere.

BOCA

Mexico City, Mexico

Design Agency **Manifiesto Mx** | Photography **Diego Davazt**

BOCA is the first dessert restaurant in Mexico City. Unlike traditional bakeries, BOCA creates a unique sensory experience where the dishes are the star of the day. Meanwhile, BOCA's menu includes exclusive desserts that invite people to rediscover the way they enjoy. The design team created a logotype with basic figures that blend naturally with interior design. They also included carefree ink stains patterns in golden finishes that reflect creativity and function as a complementary element within the restaurant.

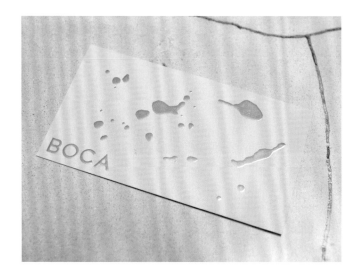

Bread Factory

Athens, Greece

Design **Luminous Design**

Bread Factory is a multi-purpose hall combining a bakery, a pastry shop, and a restaurant. While keeping the concept of the factory, the designers chose an abstract path to create a bold logo. That allowed them more freedom and flexibility on its uses. Alongside this, they selected a stylish colour palette that enhances the formation of an easily discernible identity. The custom, double-width typography they created expresses the handcrafted procedure of the brand's offerings.

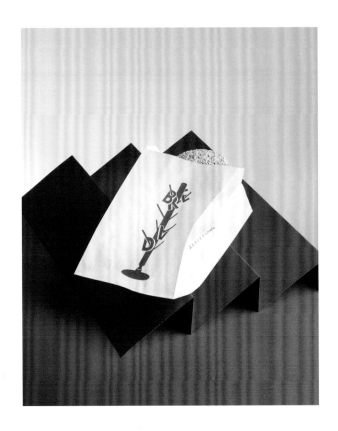

Wantadream

Fuzhou, China

Design Agency **Temperature up up up**
Design **Liang Jia, Huang Liyan**

Wantadream is also known as Goodnight Dessert. The designers hope to give the brand a new meaning through simple dismantling in English words and leave a gap-filling to the dessert makers and the dessert consumers. Meanwhile, the colon in the visual identity shows the concept of expression and need. It emphasises sharing and communication.

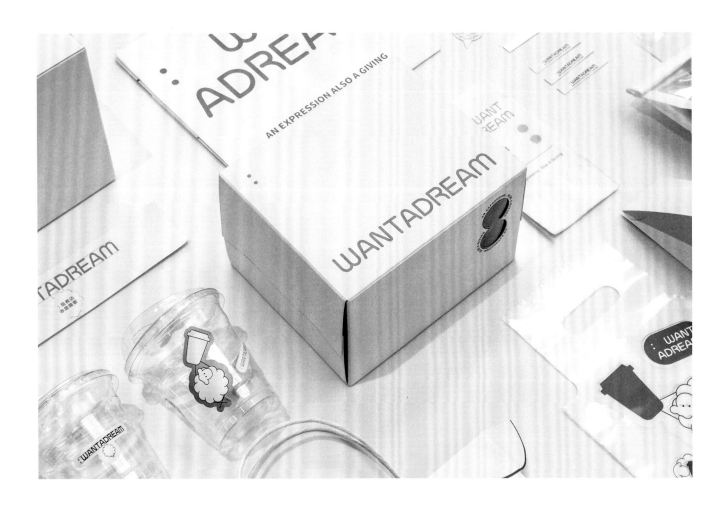

CRU+

Melbourne, Australia

Design Agency **Hue Studio** | Creative Direction **Vian Risanto**
Design **Vian Risanto, Vania Japri, Mariana Judiarti**

Being a sister cafe of The Crux & Co., the designers came up with the name CRU+. It is a deconstructed cafe offering speciality dessert and patisserie located in the Glen Shopping Centre. The design concept behind CRU+ was to create a cafe brand as a reflection of the luxurious fashion and lifestyle labels that surround CRU+. The designers combined economical paper material with printing techniques to achieve high-end finishes for desserts and coffee. The designers also collaborated with Architects Eat, which deconstructed the typical boxes in the kiosk, creating an arrangement of bespoke joinery and signages without barriers.

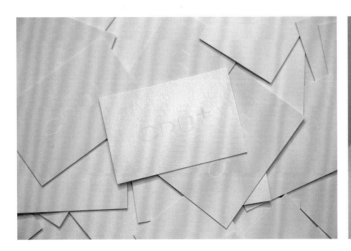

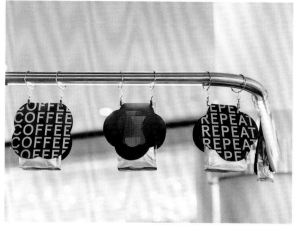

Antoinette Cake Shop

Mexico City, Mexico

Design **Matías Funes** | Collaboration **Cantera Estudio**

The main goal of this project is to emphasise the craftsmanship concept, Matías decided to use the engraving technique to give it a rustic and warm feeling while preserving the elegance and sophistication of the establishment and the iconic figure that represents. The blue tone was used to modernise the brand and add the pastel shades to express softness. The graphic symbol in the logo is the abstraction of the famous Austrian archduchess princess Marie Antoinette. Antoinette's connection with patisseries is reinforced with the famous phrase "Qu'ils mangent de la brioche (Let them eat cakes)."

Index

\\' Brand Agency

workbyw.com

\\' supports client's business ambition through branding activities. Their aim is none other than to create a meaningful brand experience at its best. They examine the real business challenges and put their best effort into the foremost solutions for the brand—sometimes they even try to push the possible limitations. Far from being a pure visual beast, they believe brand experience is determined by its soul and purpose.

7654321STUDIO

behance.net/7654321studio

7654321STUDIO, an independent creative design integration service studio, fully interprets the brand and seeks a logical way, through visual communication, using different media to convey information, allowing the brand to dialogue with consumers. As an idea creator and storyteller, 7654321STUDIO provides design consulting services for clients in various fields.

Abio Design

abio.cc

Abio Design creates humane solutions with a purpose for business, connecting all its audiences through valuable experiences.

AguWu

behance.net/aguwu

AguWu is a Polish graphic designer focusing on branding. She has been working in this field for around a decade and has developed her unique style based on minimal, geometric shapes and playful, yet elegant designs. Such an impactful style is versatile, so her clients span over multiple industries and she is able to accommodate diverse needs of their brands.

Aleksandra Lampart

alelampart.pl

Aleksandra Lampart is a graphic designer based in Poland.

Alien Wu

behance.net/wuhaolun

Alien Wu is a graphic designer. He is good at transforming his aesthetic experience into a unique visual vocabulary. His works involve visual identity, exhibition visual design, product packaging, bookbinding, etc. From 2018 to 2021, he worked as a visual researcher at Odd Institute. His works have been included in the *Asia Pacific Design* and won a Golden Pin Design Award.

Alter

alter.com.au

Alter is a Melbourne-based design studio headed by Jonathan Wallace.

Ana Patron Toffano

behance.net/anapatron

Ana Patron Toffano is a Mexican graphic designer and illustrator.

Asís

weareasis.co

Asis is a graphic design studio based in Buenos Aires, Argentina. They work worldwide, founded and directed by Francisco Andriani and Clara Fernández, with the ability to adapt and create personalised creative good-looking solutions tailored to each project.

Astakhova Elena

behance.net/astlena

Astakhova Elena is a Russian designer focusing on naming, brand identities, and illustrations.

Atelier NOA

tinyurl.com/ateliernoa

Atelier NOA is a design studio based in Beijing and Xiamen.

Atipo®

atipo.es

Atipo® is a small studio located in Gijón, Spain set up by Raúl García del Pomar and Ismael González in the beginning of 2010. They met while studying fine arts at the University of Salamanca. Their background in fine arts allows them to combine different disciplines and produce each work through experimentation.

Autumn Studio

autumn.studio

Autumn Studio believes good design can stand the test of time. Their passion is creating meaningful work that sparks a connection with people. They help their clients build brands that they love and resonate with their unique voice. By driving authentic and considered work, they create designs that are both timeless and unexpected.

Blok Design

blokdesign.com

Blok Design collaborates with thinkers and creators from all over the world, taking on projects that blend cultural awareness, their love of art, and their belief in humanity to advance society and business alike. They work across media and disciplines, including strategy, identity, product, packaging, editorial design, websites, digital experiences, exhibitions, installations, and direction with a ferocious passion.

Both

both.studio

Both is a branding and visual communication studio co-founded by Sigiriya Brown and Dan Smith in Melbourne, Australia in 2010.

Brand Brothers

brandbrothers.fr/en

Brand Brothers is a French graphic design studio. They do brand strategy, visual identity, typography, and branding.

Bruch—Idee & Form

studiobruch.com

Bruch—Idee & Form is a nationally and internationally awarded design studio based in Graz, Austria. They develop visual design concepts and strategies in the fields of branding, editorial design, packaging and signage.

Carla Almeida, Bernardo Braga

carlaalmeida.com
behance.net/bernardobraga

Carla Almeida was born in Porto, Portugal. She has been working as an independent design and art director and university lecturer since 2003. In 2015, she decided to leap in her career and moved to Hong Kong, China. Before Prophet and Superunion (formerly known as Brand Union), she was a design director at Eight Partnership in Hong Kong and worked as a freelancer for Landor.
Bernardo Braga is a 28-year-old multidisciplinary designer based in Porto, Portugal. With a double degree in Sound & Image from Universidade Católica do Porto (2013) and in Communication Design from ESAD (2018), he is currently working in a communication agency with a focus on branding.

cheeer STUDIO

cheeerstudio.com

Cheeer STUDIO is a multidisciplinary design studio based in Beijing, China. They concentrate on exploring the edge of visual language.

Choice Studio

choice.studio

Choice Studio is a brand design studio. They offer conscious solutions under the sauce of creativity.

Cohe Studio

cohe.studio

Based in Hanoi, born in its deep-rooted culture, Cohe is a design studio that focuses on the story and emotion behind each project.

Daniela Arcila

danielaarcila.com

Daniela Arcila is a Mexican graphic designer. She is a strong believer that good design is all about good research and details.

David Barath Design

davidbarath.com

David Barath Design is a Hungarian studio specialising in branding and identity design.

democràcia estudi

democraciaestudio.com

Established in València, Spain since 2011, democràcia estudi is a collaborative project which develops branding through visual language.
democràcia estudi thinks and creates global brand experiences, and ideas to change the world.
Using design as a basis, they project images and objects always through a concept with their own graphic identity.

Design Studio B.O.B.

designstudio-bob.com

Design Studio B.O.B. is an independent agency for design, packaging, and illustration that works internationally with offices in Düsseldorf and Berlin. They believe that design should be honest, smart, and fun and made with love in every detail. Their focus lies on a social, environmental, and socially responsible design that has a unique look and points out the strength of each of their clients.

Elisabetta Vedovato

elisabettavedovato.com

Elisabetta Vedovato is a graphic designer and illustrator who communicates better with images than words. She is a versatile creative interested in everything visual. She spends her days looking for the beauty of all kinds. She trusts in the impressive power of aesthetics, especially when combined with meanings and stories.

Eskader, Aces of Space

eskader.be
acesofspace.com

Eskader is the Belgium-based studio of Fre Lemmens with more than a decade of experience in graphic design, illustration, branding, and much more.
Aces of Space is a flexible team. They are team players, creators, and thinkers, complementing each other, aligning their powers for the greatest possible efficiency and effect, always custom-fit to each and every project.

Estudio Albino

estudioalbino.com

Estudio Albino is a concept of possibilities. It is a blank sheet from where the ideas of their clients come true. It is not just about naming a product, making an identity or packaging, but about telling the stories relevant for a brand to impact people's lives.

Estudio Nuar

estudionuar.com

Estudio Nuar is a boutique creative studio specialising in branding.

Fable

fable.sg

Fable is an award-winning design consultancy from Singapore with an international footprint. They work across brand identities, experiences, and typography.

FAENA STUDIO

faena-studio.org

FAENA is a graphic design studio specialising in communication and branding. They materialise concepts in projects with a solid and transcendent language. Their design approach is defined by a strategic development driven by a value, an aesthetic and a deep understanding of language and communication.

For The People

forthepeople.agency

For The People acknowledges the First Peoples of Australia, their elders past, present, and emerging. They pay their respects to the traditional storytellers, designers, artists, and owners of the land where they live and work.

Foreign Policy Design Group

foreignpolicy.design

Foreign Policy Design Group is a team of idea makers & storytellers who help clients and brands realise and evolve their brands with creative and strategic deployment of traditional terrestrial channel and digital media channels. Led by creative directors Yah-Leng Yu and Arthur Chin, the group works on a good smorgasbord of projects, such as creative/art direction and design, branding, brand strategy, digital strategy, strategic research, marketing campaign services for luxury fashion, lifestyle brands, fast-moving consumer goods brands, arts and cultural institution, and think tank consultancies.

FUGA Studio

fugastudio.it

FUGA is an independent visual arts studio based in Rome, Italy. In 2019, after years of working side by side in a well-known Italian agency, Giulia Santopadre and Viola Moroni, with their opposite personalities and complementary design skills, founded FUGA Studio. Since then, they have worked on projects ranging from branding to packaging to editorial design, with a pivot on the food and beverage industry and an exceedingly keen eye on typography.

Futura

byfutura.com

Futura is a creative studio and wants to change the world. They wish they could find the cure for cancer but they will not. Instead, they create great brands, provocative images, beautiful objects, comfortable spaces, and user-friendly interfaces. That is their way of improving the quality of life for those they reach.

Giovanni Borde

gioborde.com

Giovanni Borde is a brand designer and visual storyteller currently working and living in Dubai. He has been working in the industry for nearly 12 years, helping brands create strong narratives to achieve recognition in the market. He believes that all brands have a story to tell. How to tell it compellingly is what makes it stands out.

Grávita

somosgravita.com

As a business branding partner, Grávita creates a positive impact on its clients' businesses through the transformation of the brands.

H3l Branding Agency

h3lag.com

H3l Branding Agency was founded in 2004 in Patagonia, Argentina. They stand out for their innovation and conceptual development. The team develops commercial and artistic projects with a worldwide impact. Their independent personality has focused on the new generations creating a new level of brandings developments.

HDU23 Lab

hdu23.design

HDU23 is a comprehensive design agency that integrates strategic planning, visual design, and space design in Wuxi, China. HDU23 Lab is its graphic design studio. They strive to provide accurate, distinctive, and differentiated graphic design services for commercial projects, and they also insist on exploring and practising in professional fields such as fonts and typography.

HeyMoon Agency

heymoon.agency

Heymoon Agency is based in Samara, Russia. Their specialisation is branding, interior, and motion design.

Hue Studio

huestudio.com.au

Hue Studio is based in Melbourne, Australia. They specialise in brand development for the hospitality, architecture, and commercial sectors. They love to solve problems with fun creativity, create effective and tailored yet functional design solutions that attract, engage, and inspire. They got awarded as Best of the Best Small Studio at the 2017 Melbourne Design Awards.

Human

byhuman.mx

Human is an independent design firm founded by Alejandro Flores in 2016. This strategic design studio has skills and experience to bring focus and clarity to each brand identity.

invade

invade.design

invade is a brand design studio based in Medellín, Colombia, that partners with dreamers to turn logic into extraordinary, striving to create successful, bold and aesthetic identities.

Karla Herdia

behance.net/karlachic

Karla Herdia is a Mexican designer. She believes in human and functional design. She tries to relate and find the best solution in each project, looking for inspiration constantly from cultures and history, buildings, nature, etc.

Karla Hernández (Charlötte)

behance.net/khm

Karla Hernández (Charlötte) is a Mexican graphic designer and illustrator. She has founded her own design studio—Sacro Studio.

Kieran Reilly, Shine Agency

kieranreilly.com
theshineagency.com

Kieran Reilly is a Glasgow-based designer with over ten years of experience in the design industry. He strives to help his clients tell their story through smart and conceptual work. His love of creation has helped build lasting relationships with clients and creatives throughout Scotland and further fields.
Shine Agency takes pride in delivering exceptional work as part of an experienced and dedicated team.

Kurt Studio

kurtstudio.com

Kurt Studio is a Russian design studio with the passion of working closely with people and businesses to help them for the creation, evolution, and reinvention of their brands.

Louis Ngo

behance.net/andrewngoo

Louis Ngo is a designer from Ho Chi Minh City, Vietnam. He specialises in coffee photography.

Luminous Design

luminous.gr

Luminous Design is an Athens-based storytelling studio. Their services include branding, brand identity, print, digital design, packaging design, and creative direction.

Lung-Hao Chiang

behance.net/st60701

Lung-Hao Chiang is a designer from Taiwan, China. He has been currently serving in the coffee industry for six years. He is accustomed to doing branding, product development, design, copywriting, and marketing planning together. He likes consumer goods more than art; life more than rituals. He loves going to the supermarket more than an exhibition, and he feels that things that are close enough to life are culture.

M — N Associates

m-n.associates

M — N Associates is a branding and creative design studio. They help create meaningful solutions and designing cool brands with powerful messages. Their approach is interdisciplinary. They are working not only to set up sustainable systems but also intelligent strategies. Their works embrace a diverse range of creative solutions across brand and graphic system, products and packaging, websites and digital experiences, architecture and interior direction.

P168–169

Manifiesto Mx

bymanifiesto.mx

Manifiesto Mx is a design studio specialising in branding. They know that ideas have the power to transform, so they transform unique ideas into memorable concepts, images, spaces, and experiences. That is their way of giving something to the world: they shape the invisible.

P064–065, 078–079, 224–225

Mantra

mantra.mx

Mantra is a creative communication agency based in Mérida, Yucatán, Mexico, passionate about design and strategy, made up of three specialised areas: branding, inbound marketing, and audiovisuals. They believe in the mantra of each project, the essence that makes it unique. They work alongside every great brand in the process of finding, conceptualising, projecting it creatively and functionally to achieve their communication objectives.

P160–161

Marka Collective

markacollective.com

The works of Marka Collective are mainly in the creative fields of logo design and brand identity. They strive to give their clients the proper attention that they deserve and help them promote and advertise their businesses to make them reMARKAble.

P148–149

Matías Funes

behance.net/matiasfunes

Matías Funes is a professional designer experienced in various fields. He considers that design is a vital part of his life. His job and commitment are to create unique concepts materialised in beautiful and functional visual experiences.

P232

meh. Design Studio

meh.pt

meh. is a creative duo based in Porto, Portugal, who loves making a difference through branding. Their mission is to take brands to the next level, so they can go from being meh. to do something extraordinary.

P094–095

Mucca

mucca.com

Mucca is a design and branding studio that combines strategic thinking and seductive design to help each brand find its voice, changing strangers into devotees, and challenges into triumphs. From startups, retailers and beauty powerhouses to various renowned hotels and restaurants, Mucca's work has bolstered its reputation as one of the industry's most respected companies.

P068–069

Néstor Bada

nestorbada.com

Néstor Bada is a Spanish multidisciplinary art director specialising in creating unique and memorable visual universes for international brands and innovative clients.

P174–175

NICE GUY

niceguy.sk

NICE GUY is a design practice with a focus on branding and visual communication.

P120–123

Parámetro Studio

parametro.studio

Parámetro Studio is directed by Cristina and Vanessa, based in Monterrey, Mexico. As a worldwide studio, they provide a fresh contemporary vision on the design that challenges the standards and pushes creativity forward. They offer various services for clients in all fields, such as art direction, brand identity, and consultancy. Their approach is based on visual and conceptual exploration performed by an interdisciplinary team with a unique sense of current culture. The studio engages in collaborations with a talented network of artists and designers to create works that stand at the forefront of visual culture.

P186–187

Pedro, Pastel & Besouro

pedropastelbesouro.com

Pedro, Pastel & Besouro started in 2014 as a multi-arts lab focusing on handcrafted techniques to develop artistic and design projects. They believe drawing is the basis of the creative process to build illustrations, graphic design, and animation projects.

P050–051

Perky Bros

perkybros.com

Established in 2009, Perky Bros exists to help brands gain clarity, value, and distinction through design. They work with startups to more established brands to create visual identities built on plain-spoken, ambitious ideas—always grounded in research and meticulously crafted in their execution.

Pocca

pocca.design

Pocca is a Shanghai-based design studio that focuses on building visual rhythm through branding and communication design to transform chaotic surroundings into long-lasting and charming episodes.

Puro Diseño

purodiseno.rocks

Puro Diseño is a branding studio based in Mérida, Mexico. They translate everything into creative language; for them, the design comes from every little moment that shapes people's life.

Sergio Laskin Agency

sergiolaskin.com

Sergio Laskin Agency is an open invitation for true collaborative partnerships with clients and talented people from all creative disciplines.

Sociedad Anónima

sociedadanonima.mx

Founded in 2006 by Rodrigo Tovar, Sociedad Anónima is a design studio focusing on creative and innovative ideas for all those who believe in the power of design as a creator of unique identities and narratives.

Sociedad Anónima is a team working from Mexico City with an international perspective and clients in several countries.

studio fnt

studiofnt.com

studio fnt is a Seoul-based graphic design studio founded in November 2006. They collect fragmented and straying thoughts and then organise and transform them into relevant forms. Their capabilities include branding for corporate business, graphic design for exhibitions and cultural arts events, and many others in various fields, sizes, and media.

Studio Ingrid Picanyol

ingridpicanyol.com

The internationally award-winning creative director Ingrid Picanyol founded his studio in 2014. The studio is based in Barcelona, but it works with clients and collaborators throughout the world. With love for working with forward-thinking clients who understand the power and influence it can have, the studio helps build brands that everyone wants to choose tomorrow.

Studio leM

studiolem.co.kr

Studio leM is a multi-disciplinary design studio. Ranging from domestic startups to international brands, they have the capacity and creativity to find the right colour for clients of every size and every country. They create a brand that will be unforgettable, remembered, and everlasting.

Studio NinetyOne

studio-ninetyone.com

Studio NinetyOne is a design agency based in the East End of London. Since 2005 they have worked with an eclectic mix of clients who understand the value of great design. They are known for creating brands full of character and heart. They believe that the right design can evoke strong emotions and help build trust and loyalty. To them, these core qualities are the key to unlock a brand's full potential. Through the strong art direction, they produce identities, design for prints, create spaces, and build digital platforms. From small start-ups to established brands, from concepts to completion, Studio NinetyOne works closely with different clients to create unique solutions.

Studio Widok

widok.studio

Studio Widok is a multidisciplinary branding studio.

Studio Woork

studiowoork.com

Studio Woork is a design studio based in Jakarta, Indonesia. Their services include branding, exhibition, print, product design, and also creative direction. They constantly independently explore the boundaries of creativity in graphic design by creating products with great value and concepts. Through the experiments with things around—nature, human, culture, and environment, they believe design will get turned into something fresh, contemporary, and bold.

StudioWMW

studiowmw.com

StudioWMW is a multidisciplinary design studio based in Hong Kong, China and founded in 2013. They create branding, prints, products, packaging, exhibitions, installations, and websites.

Suprematika

suprematika.ru

Suprematika creates the identity, graphics, and websites. And they do them well. Since 2009, they have invented and implemented hundreds of projects and have won nearly every festival award in the CIS and Europe, and finally became the second top branding agency in Russia.

Tangible Design

tangiblebd.com

Tangible is an expert in design strategy, brand design, and verbal branding. They provide an integrated solution to brand issues.

Tats Oquendo, Tavo Gómez

behance.net/tatsoquendo
behance.net/tavogomez

Tats Oquendo is a Colombian graphic designer currently working in art direction, branding, illustration, and UI design. Tavo Gómez is a Colombian graphic designer currently working in branding and advertising campaigns.

Temperature up up up

weibo.com/u/7395187931

Temperature up up up is a design studio based in Fuzhou, China.

The Colour Club

thecolourclub.com.au

The Colour Club is a design studio specialising in branding, packaging, and creative direction.

The Lab Saigon

thelabsaigon.com

The Lab Saigon is a company of creative professionals in strategy, identity, spatial design, communication, and emerging media.

Thinking Room

thinkingroominc.com

Thinking Room is a comprehensive branding and graphic design company to make things that matter since 2005. They think and craft ideas that span across multiple mediums: identities, campaigns, strategies, websites, prints, editorials, spaces, and many others that go far beyond the label.

Tiare Hernández Payano

behance.net/thiare

Tiare Hernández Payano is an independent designer from the Dominican Republic.

Tux Creative Co

tux.co

Tux is more than a traditional agency. It's a creative company under one roof with 75 talents and five expertises. Tux has demonstrated its leadership in sustainability, governance, as well as environmental and community engagement.

VVORKROOM

vvorkroom.com

VVORKROOM is a creative studio based in Barcelona and Mexico City, specialising in branding and strategy with a distinctly human approach.

Where's Gut Studio

wheresgut.com

Founded in 2018, Where's Gut is a graphic design studio named after the studio's cat—Gut, which means luck and tangerine in Cantonese. They practice design through strategic storytelling to achieve practical solutions, which are timeless and engaging. Working collaboratively with brands and organisations, they want to create a visual language that communicates who they are and simultaneously clarifies what they are.

Wunder Werkz

iheartwunderwerkz.com

Wunder Werkz is a design studio working with multi-disciplinary materials, mediums, and methods to create unique brand outcomes.

Acknowledgment

....

We would like to express our gratitude to all of the designers and agencies for their generous contribution of images, ideas and concepts. We are also very grateful to many other people whose names do not appear in the credits, but who have made specific contributions and provided support. Without them, the successful compilation of this book would not have been possible. Special thanks to all of the contributors for sharing their innovation and creativity with all of our readers around the world.

....